GREAT APE ODYSSEY

GREAT APE ODYSSEY

BY DR. BIRUTÉ MARY GALDIKAS | PHOTOGRAPHS BY KARL AMMANN | FOREWORD BY JANE GOODALL

ABRAMS, NEW YORK

TABLE OF CONTENTS

ACKNOWLEDGMENTS

FIRST OF ALL, I WISH TO THANK the government of the Republic of Indonesia and its officials for their continued strong support of the Orangutan Foundation International's (OFI) and my mission: the late Minister Soesilo Sudarman, former Minister Ali Alatas, former Minister Joop Ave, former Minister Djamaludin Suryohadikusomo, former Minister Sarwono Kusumaatmadja, former Ambassador Abdul Rachman Ramly, former Ambassador Arifin Siregar, the late Minister Soedjarwo, former Minister Prof. Emil Salim, Mr. Sunten Manurang, former Minister Doro Djatun Kuntjoro-Jakti, and the late Minister Sumitro Djojohadikusumo, who helped establish Orangutan Foundation Indonesia. I also thank former Ambassador Fanny Habibie, the late Chief of Police Hoegeng, the late General Rachman Masjhur, and former President Megawati Sukarnoputri. In addition, my deep gratitude goes to the provincial government of Kalimantan Tengah, especially former Governor W. Gara; my first adopted parent, the late Assistant to the Governor, G. Binti; former Governor Sylvanus; former Governor Gatot Amrih; the current Governor and Vice-Governor; and to the former and current Regents (Bupati) of Kotwaringin Barat, including Pak Dharman.

For their great patience and understanding I thank my family: my husband Pak Bohap bin Jalan; my parents, Filomena Galdikas and the late Antanas Galdikas; my sister, Aldona Galdikas-Franz; and my children, Binti, Fred, and Jane.

My sincere gratitude is extended to OFI Board members and former members: Dr. Nancy Briggs, Albertino Abela, John Beal, Suzy Dorr, Ashley Leiman, Caroline Gabel, Steven

PAGE 1
An immature gracile chimpanzee, or bonobo, gazes out serenely into a forest world that is in danger of disappearing forever. Bonobos are found in only one country, Democratic Republic of Congo (DRC), and are the most endangered of the African great ape species.

PAGE 2
Swinging away, a teenage gracile chimpanzee, or bonobo, has fun at a sanctuary in DRC. Like their cousins, the robust chimpanzees, bonobos seem very much at home both in the trees and on the ground.

PAGE 4
The sun rises on the rain forests of southeastern Cameroon in West Africa. The African tropical rain forest formation is smaller in area than the rain forests of the Amazon and Southeast Asia. Nonetheless, this forest in Cameroon teems with life, including two of the four species of great apes, the robust chimpanzee and the gorilla.

PAGE 5
A 600-foot-long bridge that links the Sekonyer Kanan River to Camp Leakey in Tanjung Puting National Park, Kalimantan Tengah, Indonesia. Built in 1975 by the provincial government of Kalimantan Tengah (Central Indonesian Borneo) to make it easier for tourists to visit Camp Leakey, the bridge has fulfilled its purpose. About a thousand visitors visit the camp annually, making this the number one tourist attraction in this isolated, remote province that until now has attracted fewer visitors than the other more populous and accessible provinces of Kalimantan.

OPPOSITE
The author, in the early 1970s, with orangutans Sugito, Rio, and Subiarso. Photograph by Rodney Brindamour.

Karbank, Dr. Gary Shapiro, Eric Raymond, Tiffany Boswell, Norman Lear, Barbara Spencer, Andy Sabin, Nancy Abraham, Gerry Sugarman, Gordon Getty, the late Blanche Whittey, Ruta Lee, and in Australia, Leif Cocks. I also thank close OFI friends such as Dr. Jane Goodall; Ed Begley; Rod and Yuni Brindamour; Stefanie Powers; Betty White Ludden; Dr. Lillian Rachlan; Dr. Amory Lovins; the late Robert Wilkie, who was the first and staunchest supporter of my work; Jonathan Wilkie, who carries on his father's tradition; Rod Briggs; Lady Gilbert; Charlotte Lowell Grimm, RN; Pak Uil Otol; Pak Oncom; the late Leighton Wilkie; Michelle Dujomovic; Andrea Gorzitze; Ralph Arbus; JunAnn Holmes; Ulle Weber; Karin Lind; Mare Tiido; Inggriani Hartanto Shapiro; Jenny Busch; Isabella Rossellini; and Julia Roberts, as well as special thanks to Georgeanne Irvine, Marcia Hobbs, Edwin Wald, Olive Kemp, Sally Spencer, Cynthia Wilford Borja, and Debra Erickson.

Extraordinary thank-yous go to Wallis Annenberg, Sallie and Rowland Perkins, Janet Leigh and Chris Hoar, Alan and Mumsey Nemiroff, and Paula Meehan Kent, as well as to Suzanne Kayne and Patricia Shenker Ttee.

I also thank: Mimi Abers, Glenda Adams, Kay Bassford, George S. Bell, Robert J. Benke, Dottie Benke, Gary Blond, Jennifer Barker, William H. Breitmeyer, Jamie Brown, Patsy Cashmore, Lisa Couturier, Helen Davis, Jim De Lara, Jack and Karen Derrico, Col. Bill Disher, Mandy Dunford, Claire Easby, Neva Folk, Debra Gamble, Carol Gee, Louise Geist, Laura Gerwitz, Cindy Gibat, Ellen Goff, Elizabeth Groat, Ralph R. Gut, Jackie Hanrahan, Lou Harrell, Valerie M. Hart, the late Al Hibbs and Marka Hibbs, Barbara Henderson, Henry Heymann, Nancy Hanson, Janet Herbruck, Judy Mansfield, Jane Maczuzack, Kathy Irwin, Kerry Jess, David Lappen, Rebecca Levine, Jan V. Levitan, Don and Margie Mennell, Audrey Mertz, Claudia Olesniczak, Carl Palassolo, Becky Keller, Carol S. Piligian, Silvia Reiche, Marty Rope, Miriam F. Shapiro, Graeme Strike, Karen Taubner, Jo Anne Tilzhman, Carol Tilton, Mirian L. Trogdon, Kimberly Wood, Tamboleyn Streeter, Rebecca Wadler, Winifred Barrows, Paul Clark, Judy Clark, Martine Collette, Dr. Richard Glassberg, Cathryn Hilker, Dr. Mark Morris, Sharon Yanish, and John Yondorf.

I also thank Jim Dugan and Michael Shabtaie of the OFI office as well as former executive director Neal Sperling and former staff member Noah Green. I am very grateful to Chris Martin, our web master. I thank Lisa Mather, Education Officer in the OF London office. I thank Lisa Brooker for her devotion. I thank the past volunteer teams and study-tour groups, which are organized out of London, especially Mike Hollis, Thomas Poole, Justin Gervais, Cara Buckley, Gale Smith, Jennifer Hile, Jo Miller, Gaye French, Stacy Weddington, and Elke Burlich and John Filomeno. I especially thank Julian Matthews of Discovery Initiatives for his vision and persistence in organizing the study tours. I thank Ian Redmond for looking over the gorilla chapter. Board member Ashley Leiman is to be congratulated on the hard work of her very productive London office.

Special thank-yous go to: Joan Embery and Duane Pillsbury, Bonnie Morrison, Violet Soo-Hoo, Serena Mitchell, Garfield Mitchell, Julian Newman and EIA, Ruby and Molly Nelson, Sara Rutherford Nichols, Sheryl Osborne, Alex Pitt, Eliot Ponchik, Diane and Colin Forkner, Nora Frazer, Harry L. Rossi, Noel Rowe, Brad Braufman, Ann Charles, Laura Debnar and Joe Schmick, Ambassador Ed and Allene Masters, Michael Charters, Dr. Jill Kusba, Susan Raisin, Glen Hori, Suzy Leonard, Andrea Birkby, Peter Knights, Jim Watt, Evelyn Gallardo and David Root, Betty Thomas, Katherine Rust, Mark Monaco, Hatsy Kniffin, Dr. Patsy Simpson, Charlotte Ross, Dr. Betsy Lyons, Glen Hori, Barbara Shaw, Maureen Taubman, Dr. Maylene Wong, Dr. Ann Zeller, Paula Adams, Allen Altcheck, Earl Holliman, the late Corazon Bryan, Drs. Ken and Jan Gordon, Bonnie Hall, Wendy Hoole, Nancy Pearlman, Patti Jones, David Augeri, John Pearson, Bill Raffin, Nick and Nancy Rutgers, Mary Smith, Mark Starowicz, Maurine Taubman, Ann Thompkins, John and Susan Thorton, Carol Ritchie, Cynthia Tsai, Sheryl Valpono, Nora Fraser, Shirley Slater, Janine Smith, Krista Brauckmann-Towns, Lori Sheeran, Becky Rose, Rosalie Gann, Suwanna Gauntlet, Peter Max, Glenn Shiigi, Vanessa Getty, Linda Wallace-Grey, and Richard and Gloria Wurman.

I thank former Universitas Nasional students: Suharto Djojosudarmo, Jaumat Dulhaja, Dr. Endang Soekara, Dr. Barita Manulang, Dr. Yatna Supriatna, Edy Hendras, Ichlas al Zackie, Yan Suriyana Wirmidjaja, Dwi Sutanto, Benny Djaya, Natusudraduat, Mahfudz Markaya, Dadang Kusmana, Richard Pattan, Pepen Abdullah, Benny Ismunadji, Toto Susilarto, Coke Gede Parthasuniya, Mudjiono, Mohammed Boang, Djoharly Debok, Undang Halim, Heru, Dayat, Maulana, Ms. Renie Djojoasmoro, Togu Simorangkir, Gatot and Ms. Ewa.

I thank my friends and staff in Pangkalan Bun, particularly Mrs. Waliyati, Mrs. Mardiana Chandra, Pak Aju, Mr. Hartani Mukti, Pak Danthe, Pak Charles, Dr. Rosa Garriga and Stephen Brend.

At SFU I thank Drs. Chuck Crawford, Richard Shutler, Phil Hobler, Eldon Yellowhorn, David Burley, Mark Skinner, Roy Carlson, John Driver and Ingrid Nystrom, Ann Sullivan, Robin Banerjee, and Andrew Barton for help and friendship, as well as my students, too numerous to name, but particularly Michael Reid, Juliet Craig, Rosemary Powers, and Tamaini Snaith.

Finally, my deepest gratitude goes to Robert Morton, Eric Himmol, Andrea Danese, and Darilyn Carnes at Harry N. Abrams, all of whom had the vision to make this book a reality, and to Ann Levine, who graciously helped edit and whose devotion to orangutans is exemplary. A special thank-you to Mike Hamilburg, who introduced me to Abrams, to Dr. Jane Goodall for the foreword, and especially to Karl Ammann, wildlife photographer extraordinaire, whose wonderful photographs of the great apes grace this volume and make it a book for all time.

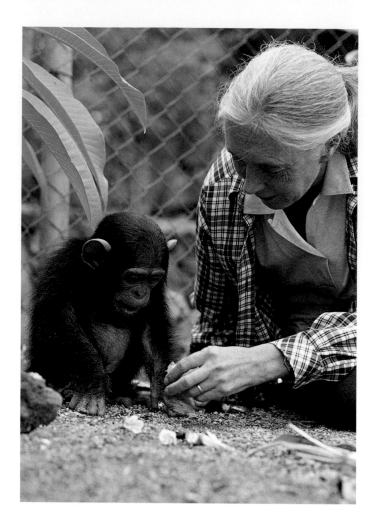

I AM DELIGHTED THAT BIRUTÉ MARY GALDIKAS, my dear friend and "Leakey sister," has written *Great Ape Odyssey* as a sequel to her previous book, the well-received *Orangutan Odyssey*. Biruté, one of the most important primatologists working in the field, has been studying, conserving, and protecting orangutans and tropical rain forest in Indonesian Borneo (Kalimantan) for the past three decades. Her pioneering work has caught the attention of the whole world. She has painstakingly documented orangutan behavior and ecology previously unknown to science and provided a long-term scientific record of an endangered species, orangutans, that will probably never again be equaled.

In *Great Ape Odyssey* Biruté turns her attention to all the great apes: chimpanzees, bonobos, gorillas, and orangutans. The great apes are our closest cousins in the animal kingdom. They possess cognitive abilities once thought to be unique to humans. They have excellent memories, exhibit foresight, self-recognition, and problem-solving capabilities, are capable of cross-modal transfer of information, generalization, and even abstract thought. Their emotions seem very similar to ours. We can recognize in them happiness, envy, anger, shame, sadness, even jealousy, and something akin to love. Like humans, they can be compassionate and altruistic on one hand but can demonstrate extremes of cruelty and brutality on the other. They are truly like us, indeed almost too much like us for their own good, as hundreds of captive chimpanzees bred for laboratory research can attest.

All this has served to blur the line, once drawn so sharply and defended so tenaciously, between humans and the great apes, as well as the rest of the animal kingdom. Once we acknowledge that not only we humans have emotions, personalities, and minds, but that great apes possess these attributes as well, it will become increasingly difficult to deny these magnificent animals the respect they so richly deserve.

Unfortunately, while some progress has been made in improving conditions for captive apes, the situation regarding ape populations in the wild is grim. The killing of apes for the bushmeat trade, the increasing commercialization of this trade, the expansion of human populations into once pristine great ape habitats, and the large-scale destruction of these habitats have endangered our close relatives and put them on the path to extinction. The situation is critical. Unless we act now on all fronts and together as individuals and organizations, all the great apes could disappear as wild populations in Africa and Asia within the next fifty years. How shameful if the time comes when only captive great apes are all that remain to represent their species. What a bleak legacy to leave behind for our grandchildren and theirs.

Biruté, Dian Fossey, and I shared the same mentor, Louis Leakey (1903–1972), the great palaeo-anthropologist whose work revised our understanding of human origins. Louis would be very proud of what Biruté has accomplished. I also know that he would be very proud of how, against great odds, Biruté has persevered and done more to protect orangutans from the threat of extinction in the wilds of Borneo than has any other single person.

In *Great Ape Odyssey* Biruté joins with Karl Ammann, who provided the photographs for the book. As a photographer, Karl is superb. Living in Africa and visiting Indonesia frequently, Karl's passion for the great apes is evident in his brilliant photographs, sometimes taken under very difficult conditions.

This book provides a fascinating look at all great ape species and documents not only their lifeways, but also the ways they are threatened with extinction. Unless we give the great apes all the attention, care, and protection we can provide, the vibrant world described on these pages is in danger of vanishing forever. My hope is that Biruté's book will serve as a call to action so that great apes will not vanish from this earth as populations in the wild, and that we humans will allow them to live in peace as they have for countless centuries. For the sake of both great apes and humans, I pray that this will be so.

INTRODUCTION: OUR BLOOD KIN, THE GREAT APES

I reject (Linnaeus') first division, which he calls Primates . . . because my vanity will not suffer me to rank humankind with apes, monkeys, and bats.

THOMAS PENNANT, 1771

If we did not know that apes and long tail monkeys . . . are not human beings but beasts, those same natural historians who pride in curious lore might with unscathed vanity foist them upon us as diverse distinct tribes of men.

ST. AUGUSTINE (354–430 CE)

THE EARLY MORNING AFRICAN SUN beat down mercilessly as I stood at the top of a brown hill gazing into the valley below where the air was still cool, the foliage lush and laden with dew. It was 1971, and I was on my way to Indonesia to study wild orangutans. My mentor, Louis Leakey, had suggested that I first spend time with Jane Goodall at Gombe National Park in Tanzania observing wild chimpanzees. Louis Leakey had also mentored Jane and felt a visit to Gombe would help prepare me for my future study. It was here at Gombe where I first met and observed great apes in the wild.

I could hear chimpanzees pant-hooting in the distance. But the chimpanzees I was observing—an adult female, Passion, and her small juvenile daughter, Pom—paid no attention. As Passion and Pom climbed out of the green valley below, they encountered Melissa and her juvenile son. Passion continued her steady pace without so much as a glance, but Pom eagerly ran to play with the other juvenile. Within a few minutes the

play got rough and Pom ran back squealing to her mother, who appeared oblivious to her daughter's distress. Steadily and methodically, Passion continued climbing the hill, while Pom struggled to catch up. Even then I wondered about Passion's seeming indifference to her daughter. Little did I know that a few years later, when Pom became an adolescent, she and her mother would launch a reign of terror on the other adult female chimpanzees of Gombe, killing and cannibalizing their infants. But I had no idea then and neither did Jane, although new evidence was beginning to indicate that chimpanzees were not as peaceable as once thought.

I was now trudging up the hill behind Passion and Pom under a lapis lazuli–blue sky. The sun was shining. I looked back at the breathtaking view across the valley—all I knew at this moment was how unspeakably privileged I was to be following a pair of wild chimpanzees in this beautiful Edenlike place where they roamed free.

Since ancient times people have obsessed about the existence of creatures similar to themselves. Wherever we have lived, in small tribes or large civilizations, we have told stories not only of ghosts, spirits, and other supernatural beings, but also of living, breathing semi-humans who inhabited this earth along with us. It was as if we knew that we were not alone. And for much of our history, we were not. As recently as 35,000 years ago there were at least two types of human beings on our planet: the last western European Neanderthals who disappeared around that time, and, in Africa and the Middle East, humans who closely resembled people living today and were probably our ancestors. Indeed, for millions of years our own early ancestors and those of our great ape cousins— chimpanzees, gorillas, and orangutans—lived side by side in the tropical woodlands and forests of Africa.

As the world became colder and drier, the ancestors of the great apes retreated with the shrinking tropical forests, whereas our ancestors eventually moved out of the forests onto the plains, savannahs, and edge woodlands. By the time modern-looking humans emerged 100,000 to 200,000 years ago, a variety of peoples of one sort or another were scattered throughout the temperate zones of Africa, Asia, and Europe, as well as the tropics of Asia and Africa. Only the high Arctic and the deepest reaches of great deserts and tropical forests were not yet breached. We now suspect that multiple lines of ances-

At peace with the world, a bonobo mother relaxes in a tree with her infant on her chest.

tral humans occupied Africa, Asia, and Europe as humans evolved. The great apes survived and even prospered because ancestral humans could not out-compete their great ape kin in the tropical rain forest.

The biblical story of creation that appears in the Book of Genesis parallels the paleontological record of human evolution. In the bible, Adam and Eve are forced to leave the Garden of Eden, much as our early human ancestors were forced out of the tropical rain forest onto the savannah as the world became colder and drier. Evolutionary evidence also confirms that a Cain did kill an Abel, in the sense that competing lineages of hominids probably played a role in the others' demise. Only recently, in evolutionary time, did the advent of *Homo sapiens* with its full arsenal of polished stone tools and horticultural techniques finally allow humans to re-penetrate and re-adapt to the depths of those same tropical rain forests they had once left behind.

But our "return" to Eden was marked by carnage, ambivalence, and misunderstanding. When we discovered the great apes, it took us centuries to understand our true relationship with our ape kin. The great apes became a mirror in which philosophers and priests, scientists and naturalists, reflected the varying beliefs, prejudices, and cosmologies of the age.

For thousands of years, Europeans lived in ignorance, unaware of humankind's tropical past and their primate brethren. Although primitive prosimians once thrived in the northern hemisphere, they went extinct tens of millions of years ago, leaving Europe without native nonhuman primates. Even the monkeys, Barbary macaques, on the Rock of Gibraltar are imports, probably brought from Africa in Roman times and, then as now, dependent on human provisions. Not until the

A small temporary encampment sits on the Sekonyer River, Borneo. A few local Melayu families from Kumai stay there, extracting raw resources such as wild rubber "jelutung," rattans, and "gembor" bark, which is used for making anti-mosquito incense, as well as fishing and snaring deer. The most lucrative resource is timber. Increasingly, traditional local people are organized by illegal logging bosses to bring out valuable timber from the forest. No doubt, the people at this settlement are also now involved.

sixteenth and seventeenth centuries did Europeans "discover" the great apes in tropical climes. Until then, apes ranked with unicorns and satyrs in European folklore and mythology.

Ancient Greek mythology describes "pygmaean races" that, like monkeys and apes, lived in the trees and were capable of making themselves invisible. The definitive work on ancient Greek zoological knowledge is Aristotle's *Historia animalium*, written in the third century BC. Aristotle mentioned only three nonhuman primates: monkeys with tails (possibly guenons, a genus of long-tailed African monkeys), baboons, and creatures called "tail-less apes." The latter were later identified as Barbary apes, even though they are not apes at all but atypical tail-less large macaque monkeys. Perhaps the ancient Greeks glimpsed Barbary macaques roaming the Mediterranean shores of North Africa. These monkeys had a much wider distribution in classical times than they do today. Almost certainly, ancient Greeks were acquainted with the African monkeys kept by their Egyptian contemporaries. Guenon-type monkeys appear often in ancient Egyptian art. In addition, the ancient Egyptians revered the male hamadryas baboon who, with his silvery leonine mane, represented Thoth, the god of scribes and scholars and the inventor of science and writing. In sacred Egyptian art, Thoth stood behind the King of Gods in divine assemblies, inspiring him to wisdom.

The first observation of great apes by Europeans occurred in 470 BC. A group of colonists from Carthage, sailing down the coast of West Africa, reported seeing large, hairy, stone-throwing creatures they called *gorillai*. Whether these *gorillai* (probably a local name) were actual gorillas is uncertain. In any case at least two thousand years would pass before Europeans again encountered what we now know as gorillas.

During ancient Roman times Pliny the Elder described many exotic, half-human creatures, including a race that hopped on one foot and another race that had, Cyclops-like, only one eye. Pliny's fantasia included the satyrs of India, which had the legs of a goat and the upper body of a human, and creatures with dog-shaped heads and furry clothing, which lived in the mountains. While it's difficult to extrapolate over millennia, the satyrs might have been based on the lanky *hanuman langurs*, monkeys the Hindus believe to be manifestations of Hanuman, the Monkey God. The different species of macaques that reside in the hills of India might have inspired Pliny's dog-faced creatures. But the Romans themselves, despite the vast boundaries of their empire and the far-flung travels of their legions, never encountered the great apes first-hand. The reason is simple. Far from the Middle Eastern and Mediterranean cradles of Western civilization, the great apes occupied the equatorial belt in Africa and Asia. For almost the entire sweep of human history and prehistory, humankind's closest living relatives were hidden in dense tropical forests of Central and Western Africa (gorillas and chimpanzees, including bonobos) and on the great

islands of Borneo and Sumatra in Southeast Asia (orangutans, the sole Asian great ape).

The great apes are similar to each other in some ways but very different in others. The black-haired agile chimpanzees represent our closest living relatives in the animal kingdom, sharing as much as 99.3 percent of our genetic material. There are at least two distinct species of chimpanzee: "common," or robust chimpanzees, and "bonobos," also known as gracile chimpanzees. Although bonobos were initially termed pygmy chimpanzees, little about them is pygmylike.

Bonobos are not shorter; rather they are more slender, with distinctive webbing between their second and third toes. All chimpanzees have prominent ears and usually weigh between 60–110 pounds in adulthood. They are quadrapedal knuckle-walkers, moving terrestrially over relatively long distances on the ground, but are also agile, skillful brachiators and climbers in the trees. Chimpanzees tend to be social and gregarious, living in large, somewhat flexible communities in the wild.

Gorillas are the largest of the great apes. Black-haired and black-skinned, they are large and powerful, weighing 150–220 pounds for females and up to 480 pounds for males in the wild. Sexual dimorphism is extreme. Not only are mature males two to three times larger than females, but they also exhibit a saggital crest of bone at the top of the skull, pronounced brow ridges, and a distinctive "saddle" of silver-gray hair on their back (hence the term "silverback" for mature males). Males also have air sacs in their throats and chests that serve as resonating chambers when they chest-beat to display their power. Ironically, gorillas are more sedate and calmer than the brittle-tempered robust chimpanzees. Bonobos engage in exuberant displays, but tend to be less aggressive than robust chimpanzees. Not as gregarious as chimpanzees, gorillas live in smaller, relatively stable families of females and young, led by one or two silverbacks.

Orangutans are the sole Asian great ape surviving into the present. They are distinguished from their African cousins by their shaggy red or orange coats, arboreal adaptations (longer arms, flexible hip joints, and hooklike hands and feet) and, in the wild, a semi-solitary (or solitary in the case of adult males) lifestyle. Unlike chimpanzees and gorillas, orangutans are primarily silent, which has earned them a reputation for shyness and wariness. The large adult males (almost 300 pounds in the wild) are twice the size of females and boast cheekpads that enlarge the appearance of the face. Males also display a throat-pouch that serves as a resonating chamber for the long call, a vocalization virtually never given by females.

For most of Western history the only "ape" known to scientists was a monkey: the Barbary macaque. In his *Historia animalium*, Aristotle had pointed out that the anatomy of the monkeys he had seen was similar to that of humans. In the second century AD, the Greek physician and philosopher

In the wild, adult orangutans are semi-solitary, but they go through a more gregarious stage as adolescents and subadults. Wild-born ex-captive orangutans, Rombe and Princess, express this social stage while sitting in chairs in front of one of the simple wooden buildings at Camp Leakey. Subadult male Rombe (left) adopted juvenile Barbara (sitting above his head), while Princess (right), the equivalent of a teenaged mother, holds her first infant, Prince. It is unusual for male orangutans to adopt, but Rombe was a very good parent to Barbara who suckled his nipples until they became unnaturally white. He also carried Barbara on his back through the trees as though he were her parent. The relationship lasted even after the pair returned to the wild.

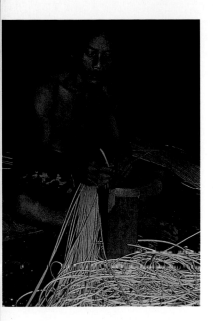

Claudius Galen applied this observation to the study of human anatomy. Given the social taboos against the use of human cadavers, Galen conducted numerous dissections and experiments on so-called lower animals, including pigs, sheep, goats, and Barbary macaques, which he considered the best substitute for humans. Galen's writings, translated first into Arabic and then later into Latin, were inaccurate because they were not based directly on internal human anatomy. However, they set the standard for Western medical theory and practice for the next thousand years. It wasn't until the mid-sixteenth century (1543) that Andreas Vesalius corrected Galen's observations by dissecting human cadavers.

During the millennium between Galen and Vesalius, the ape (actually a monkey) entered European thought and theology as a monstrous caricature of the human condition. Medieval Christian theology singled out the Barbary macaque as a diabolical creature whose lack of a tail took on metaphysical significance. A tail was thought to be a necessary component of all animals' anatomy. God had removed Adam's tail at Creation. Thus our lack of a tail was a sign of the unique place of humans at the apex of God's creation. By twisted logic, the hapless Barbary macaque's lack of a tail was interpreted as evidence of its imposter status and its fiendish attempt and presumption to rise above its animal status. Its grotesque nature was considered a sign of its fall from God's grace. In modern terms, it was an evil poseur.

Europe is a small, relatively isolated peninsular continent jutting out into the cold Atlantic Ocean. Relative to other continents, Europe is poor in flora and fauna. For example, Britain has only 34 native species of trees, whereas hundreds, if not thousands of native tree species thrive on tropical islands such as Borneo. Only in the fifteenth and sixteenth centuries did Portuguese and Spanish navigators open the world in all its diversity to European explorers. Before the fifteenth century with the older square-riggers, which sailed "before" the wind, journeys were long and the routes circuitous. Sailors hugged the shore. The Vikings reached the New World but could not maintain colonies because the journey back and forth to Europe was too arduous. In the fifteenth century the development of "tacking to the wind" allowed European explorers and adventurers to travel far beyond the horizon and return home relatively quickly after their voyages of discovery. Suddenly, Europe was flooded not only with the gold and silver of conquered Aztec and Inca empires, trade goods from China and India, as well as gold, ivory and (later) slaves from Africa, but the explorers and conquerors brought back plants and animals from the newly discovered tropical world.

The sheer number and variety of specimens arriving from the tropics practically overwhelmed nascent Western science. In the eighteenth century the great Swedish botanist Carolus Linnaeus devised a binomial classification system, still used

today, to make sense of nature's gradation and to systematize the abundance of tropical fauna and flora accumulating in museums and institutions of higher learning. Linnaeus grouped all living creatures—plants and animals—according to their physical similarities. He postulated a hierarchy of beings from the simplest to the most complex, culminating with humans. The hierarchy within his taxonomy begins for each animal and plant with the largest grouping and continues to the smallest: Kingdom, Phylum, Class, Order, Family, Genus, Species. He put monkeys, apes, and humans in the same order, *Primates* (which means "first"), along with bats, which were eventually removed in one of his many revisions of the system. Like his contemporaries, Linnaeus believed that the Great Chain of Being was the result of divine creation and was, therefore, perfect and immutable. Even so, Linnaeus was criticized harshly by other naturalists for both ignoring the intellectual superiority of humans and their dualistic nature—*between the beasts and the angels*—in his treatment of primates.

The printing press helped not only to propagate scientific knowledge of tropical plants and animals but also to spread explorers' tales of exotic places and peoples. Travelers' diaries and stories collected from sailors, soldiers, and sea captains were among the bestsellers of their day, fueling curiosity and wonder. In 1625 Andrew Battell, an Englishman who had been imprisoned by the Portuguese in West Africa, published his memoirs, which included what was probably the earliest description of gorillas and chimpanzees as "two kinds of Monsters, which are common in these woods and dangerous." Battell labeled these creatures as *Pongo* (gorilla) and *Engecko* (chimpanzee) and included a brief mention of "pigmey Pongokillers." Shakespeare's Caliban, a hybrid of human and beast, may have been inspired by Battell's so-called monsters.

Among the first wildlife specimens brought to Europe, alive or dead, were great apes. In 1641, Dutch anatomist Nicholaes Tulp (coincidentally the subject of one of Rembrandt's greatest paintings) provided the first detailed anatomical description of an ape. The live ape from Angola had been given to Frederick Henry, the Prince of Orange, ruler of the Netherlands. Tulp described the ape as an "Indian satyr," harking back to Pliny, but noted that the animal was called *orang-outang* by natives in the ape's land of origin because of its human-looking face. *Orang* in Malay means "person." He classified the ape as *Homo sylvestris* ("person of the woods" in Latin), *Orang-outang* (which also means "person of the forest" in Malay). In retrospect, Tulp's description and drawings suggest that the ape was not an orangutan but more likely a bonobo. The ape had webbing between his second and third toes, a characteristic common to bonobos and rarely reported in orangutans. It is deliciously ironic that the first great ape to be described by Western science happened to be the last species of great ape to be recognized by Western science in the twentieth century.

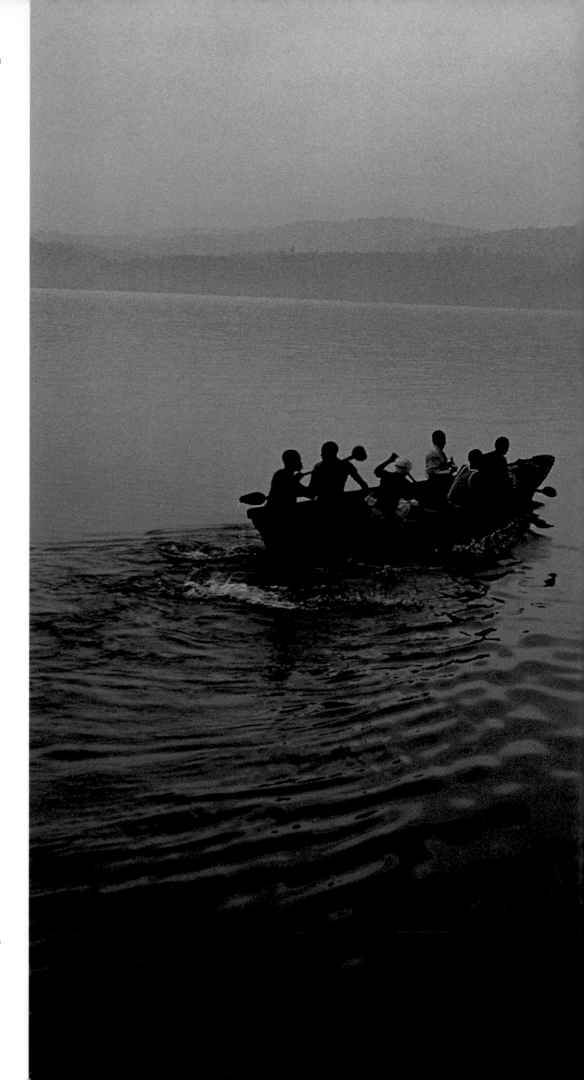

Only in 1933 did Harold Coolidge (a nephew of President Calvin Coolidge) designate bonobos as *Pan paniscus*, differentiating them from the robust chimpanzees, *Pan troglodytes*.

The first confirmed mention of a real orangutan in Western science came in 1658 when Jacob Bontius, another Dutchman, described a female orangutan as a "wonderful monster with a human face" in whom "nothing human was lacking but speech." Bontius noted that Asian natives in her place of origin believed that orangutans could actually speak but chose not to do so, for fear that they would be forced to work. Bontius used Tulp's terminology, also calling the orangutan *Homo sylvestris*. His illustration of the orangutan resembled nothing more than a rather hairy yet shapely nude woman with a beard.

The number of great ape infants and juveniles that might have died on European ships during the age of exploration is unknown, but it is probably quite large. In the closing years of the seventeenth century, the first known live ape reached the British Isles, a chimpanzee infant who died soon after arrival. In 1699, Edward Tyson, who had dissected the chimpanzee infant, published his findings in a book entitled "Orang-outang . . . or the Anatomy of a Pygmie compared with that of a Monkey, an Ape or a Man," adding pygmie to the designation of *orang-outang*. Tyson's confusion was understandable. Tales of semi-human pygmies had circulated in Europe since ancient Greek colonists had sailed down the coast of West Africa thousands of years earlier, so Tyson speculated that animals like the infant chimpanzee and the adult bonobo described by Tulp were members of the same species.

Rejecting the term satyr, Tyson placed his little "pygmie" somewhere between monkeys and humans in the Great Chain of Being that, in Western Christian thought, resulted from a single act of creation by an omnipotent God. However, his careful dissection demonstrated that, anatomically, apes are much more like humans than they are like monkeys. A creationist typical of his time, Tyson would probably have been horrified to know that he helped prepare the way for Charles Darwin's theory of evolution.

Confusion regarding the great apes remained rife. For more than a century to come, variations of the Malay name for orangutans continued to be applied to all the great apes, both African and Asian. Furthermore, the modern distinction between "monkeys" and "apes" was not yet recognized. To a

Crossing Lake Kivu between Rwanda and eastern DRC, a small boatload of locals demonstrates the porous nature of borders in Africa.

large degree, the words *monkey* and *ape* were synonymous. Any tail-less or short-tailed monkey was pronounced an ape. Travelers' and adventurers' accounts, which mixed direct observations, secondhand descriptions, folktales learned from local peoples, and sometimes imaginings, merely added to the confusion.

In 1714, however, English sea captain Daniel Beeckman published a surprisingly objective portrait of the orangutans encountered in their native islands. He described "oran-ootans" as having "larger arms than men" and "tolerable good Faces." He continued: "nimble footed and mighty strong, they throw great stones…(and) sticks at those persons who offend them," a relatively accurate description of disturbed orangutans who throw down branches from trees when annoyed. Unfortunately, Beeckman's pet orangutan infant died after seven months in captivity and never reached Europe. Almost three hundred years later, in the twenty-first century, the lifespan of many captive orangutan infants on Borneo and Sumatra is similar.

During the eighteenth and early nineteenth centuries, Westerners continued struggling to sort out the real from the imaginary. The specimens available for study were chimpanzees from West Africa and orangutans from Southeast Asia. Local people's descriptions of gorillas remained rumors. Not surprisingly, the great French naturalist Comte Georges-Louis de Buffon concluded, on the basis of the available evidence, that there was only one species of ape, which varied in size. He called the small ones (including Tulp's bonobo and Tyson's chimpanzee infant) Jockos and the large ones (orangutans and the legendary gorillas) Pongos. Others classified great apes by color, concluding that there were two types of orangutans: a black one from Africa and a red one from Asia. The black one was the robust chimpanzee and the red one the orangutan. After an intensive study of orangutan specimens, the Dutch anatomist Pieter Camper concluded that chimpanzees and orangutans were different species and that accounts of the orangutan's abilities were exaggerated. He noted that not only did orangutans lack the anatomy for speech, but also for sustained erect posture on the ground.

Even so, orangutans continued to confuse. The native Dayaks of Borneo believed that there are different types of orangutans. Many Dayak groups had different names for adult male orangutans as opposed to the smaller adult females and subadult males; other Dayaks also differentiated among adult males based on the characteristics of their cheekpads. Some believed that adult male orangutans, with their enormous size, bulging throat pouches, and ground locomotion were actually ghosts, unlike the more exclusively tree-living females. This view is understandable. Without claws or hooves, a male orangutan walking on his fists or palms on the ground makes no noise and does not give himself away in the deep gloom of the forest understory until he is almost upon an unwary individual.

Baskets heavy with produce, villagers returning home from the market balance pots and bowls on their heads on the DRC side of the Virunga Volcanoes, home of the mountain gorillas. Fortunately, mountain gorillas are not yet threatened by the bushmeat trade or the newly emerging infectious diseases such as Ebola that are wiping out chimpanzee and gorilla populations elsewhere in Africa. However, mountain gorillas are severely threatened by wars that bring large armed refugee populations into their area, death by traps meant for other species, and destruction of habitat that pushes the mountain gorillas farther up the slopes of the volcanoes into areas where survival is difficult.

Likewise, he can just as easily disappear by silently running away. Anyone who is suddenly faced with an adult male orangutan silently appearing and then seemingly vaporizing on the forest floor, can readily appreciate the belief that orangutan males are ghosts. For many years Western naturalists assumed that several species of orangutans must exist.

At the end of the eighteenth century (1779) the distinguished German anatomist Johann Blumenbach expanded on the Linnaean anatomical approach to taxonomy by adopting a more functional approach. Blumenbach concluded that the human skeleton was unique because of the many features that contribute to upright bipedal locomotion on the ground. Although apes were almost invariably depicted as walking upright on their back legs, Blumenbach showed that anatomically this would be difficult for them to sustain for long periods of time. Unlike Linnaeus, Blumenbach separated human beings from the rest of the primate family (apes and monkeys), assigning humans to their own separate family and genus called *Homo*, recognizing only one species. He dismissed the other species of *Homo* (Linnaeus had recognized four) as myths or mistakes.

Whether this separation was an over-reaction remains a subject for debate. Certainly, all scientists agree that only one species of human exists on earth today. Nonetheless, there has always been a feeling that humans, despite their undeniable distinctions, are not unique enough to be separated out definitively from the other apes, especially at the family level. (Jared Diamond, a biologist from the University of California, for one, has proposed reuniting chimpanzees and humans in a single genus. Jared classifies humans as the "third chimpanzee.")

This is what Charles Darwin knew and feared. Darwin initially developed his theory of evolution and deposited his first exposition in a sealed envelope, to be published only upon his death because he understood the ramifications of his theory to faith and society. The idea that evolution is an ongoing process of adaptation between creatures and their habitats challenged belief in a single act of Divine Creation. His theory could also be applied to society: If the natural world is not fixed and immutable, so the existing social order might change—political dynamite in Victorian England. His fear of the consequences of his findings held him back and made him hesitate. Then Darwin received a letter from Alfred Russel Wallace, an amateur naturalist traveling through the Indonesian archipelago. Wallace's essay from the tropics, which indicated that Wallace was thinking along similar evolutionary lines and was eager to publish, finally pushed Darwin to take the final step toward publishing his own work. His ambivalence remained even after his decision to publish; he commented that he felt like he was committing a murder.

In 1859 the publication of Charles Darwin's book *On the Origin of Species by Means of Natural Selection* electrified the

Western world. It offered an entirely new way of looking at human origins and provided an alternative explanation for the order in the natural world, views that seemingly excluded the Biblical description of creation. Although Darwin's volume actually contained only one sentence (and the closing sentence at that) suggesting that evolution might shed light on human origins, that sentence (elaborated on in *The Descent of Man* in 1871) was enough to kindle the fires of indignation and controversy. In 1863 T. H. Huxley, known as "Darwin's bulldog" for his fierce defense of Darwin's evolutionary theory, took Tyson's demonstrated affinity between humans and apes one step further when he cautiously suggested that not only were apes similar to humans anatomically but also behaviorally.

Huxley fought the last major campaign in Western science, concerning the close relationship between apes and humans. After he was done, no one challenged the concept that apes were closer to humans than they were to monkeys, despite the fact that they look similar in many ways to monkeys than they do to us. Indeed, to the untrained eye, apes and monkeys can be quite difficult to tell apart.

Darwin and Huxley annihilated the argument that apes are similar to humans merely by their proximity in the Great Chain of Being. Before the Darwinian revolution, humankind's inexorably superior position in the universe had been assured with a special act of creation by an omnipotent deity. Now, thanks to Darwin, the revelations of evolutionary theory indicated that apes are similar to us because we once shared a common ancestor. They are similar because we are blood kin.

While Western civilization generally accepted Darwin's thesis, many remained uneasy with this newly discovered next of kin. A new means had to be found to draw a line between ourselves and the beasts, particularly the great apes. To demonstrate human preeminence, the great apes had to be repudiated and vilified. Victorian elitism and self-importance justified the elevation of so-called civilized Europeans above their close kin, whether human or ape. The concept of the "noble savage" (including both apes and humans), which had been intellectually dominant during the Enlightenment in the eighteenth century, lost its appeal. Suddenly, a rather medieval attitude toward the apes was awakened.

From the mid-nineteenth century onward, the image of apes in Victorian culture became increasingly savage and brutal. Edgar Allan Poe used a monster ape image in *The Murders in the Rue Morgue* (1847), the first modern detective story. He described the villain, who brutally killed two women, as a creature "of an agility astounding, a strength superhuman, a ferocity brutal, a butchery without motive, a grotesquerie in horror absolutely alien from humanity." In Poe's story, the identity of the brute (in today's terminology a serial killer) is revealed when the finger marks on the throat of one of the victims perfectly matches the measurements of an orangutan's hand.

This monster image reappears in the tales of the American explorer and journalist Paul Du Chaillu, who visited Africa in the 1850s. Du Chaillu thrilled readers with his accounts of charging adult male gorillas, which he slaughtered by the score. Gorillas, he wrote, were "some hellish dreamlike creature—a being of that hideous order, half-man, half-beast," confirming in the minds of many the image of a fiend from the depths of Hades, a creature whose failure to attain human status was a sign of failure in the evolutionary scheme. A variation of this brutal ape image appeared in 1914 with the publication of Edgar Rice Burroughs's *Tarzan of the Apes*:

> The ape was a great bull weighing probably three hundred pounds. His nasty, close-set eyes gleamed hatred from beneath his shaggy brows, while his great canine fangs were bared in a horrible snarl as he paused a moment before his prey. . . . With a wild scream, he was upon her, tearing a great piece from her side . . . and striking her viciously . . . until her skull was crushed to jelly. . . . Standing erect he threw his head far back . . . and emitted his fearful roaring shriek.

Great apes got a respite from vilification in the myth-making capital of the modern world, Hollywood, when a series of Tarzan movies showed the hero becoming pals with a benign juvenile chimpanzee.

The monster image reemerged in the enormously popular film, *King Kong* (1933), which drew larger audiences than any other film released that year and remains a movie classic today. Although the ape in the film most closely resembled a gorilla, neither chimpanzees nor orangutans escaped this terrifying characterization. King Kong became the proverbial ape for audiences around the world. Even then, Western science had no idea that gorillas are peaceful vegetarians, and that the male silverbacks who terrorized movie audiences are exceptionally tender fathers.

Not until the middle of the twentieth century did perceptions of great apes begin to change. The years following World War II brought unprecedented prosperity to North America. With Europe still recovering from the ravages of war and many African and Asian nations breaking the fetters of colonialism, the United States and Canada entered an era of comfortable domesticity, with easy employment for most people and a car in every garage. In the early 1960s, a new generation declared its opposition to a different kind of war and its desire to return to nature and simplicity. "Flower power" was a catch phrase and "make love, not war" became the rallying cry of a generation opposed to the aggressive materialism of "the establishment" and the conventionality of their parents' generation. Now humans were seen as killer apes, in Desmond Morris's phrase, and the real great apes became idealized.

The intensity of male chimpanzees interacting at Chimfunshi Sanctuary is unmistakable. Studies of wild chimpanzees indicate that male chimpanzees may associate more closely with each other than with females, as dominance frequently depends on the establishment and maintenance of alliances and friendships among adult males.

The ape to benefit most from this new ethos was the robust chimpanzee. Jane Goodall's and British primatologist Vernon Reynold's preliminary reports of gentle, peaceable (albeit noisy) chimpanzees living in open societies in an Edenlike environment supported popular societal aspirations of the times. And Jane Goodall's discovery that robust chimpanzees use and make tools merely enhanced the flower-child image. The new generation cheered the news that chimpanzees were, after all, "just like us"—or how we wanted to be, once again in Eden. In addition, Jane Goodall looked upon chimpanzees as distinct individuals and family members, bypassing the scientific convention of generalizing about *the* (male, female, or juvenile) chimpanzee and assigning them names rather than numbers. *National Geographic* articles, books, and Hugo van Lawick's films introduced a large popular audience to Flo and David Greybeard, as well as Melissa, Passion, and Pom, whom I had observed myself at Gombe. Ironically, ongoing research revealed that male chimpanzees are prone to intercommunity aggression (rudimentary war), predation (hunting and eating flesh), and infanticide.

Meanwhile, Louis and Mary Leakey's discovery of prehuman fossils (*Zinjanthropus, Homo habilis*) in East Africa—announced with Louis Leakey's usual flair—had engendered in the new generation a visceral acceptance of human evolution as a process from which modern humans emerged, over time, from apelike ancestors. Chimpanzees, our closest living relatives in the animal kingdom, became a model for the creature, known only from incomplete fossil skeletons, from which humans descended. Louis Leakey encouraged Jane Goodall to study robust chimpanzees at Gombe as a way of extrapolating from living creatures the lifestyle of the ancient hominids whose remains he and Mary Leakey had found in the dry valleys of Olduvai Gorge. The lush setting of Gombe—low hills with

The eyes of a male chimpanzee reflect the intelligence and emotional complexity of a creature that shares approximately 99 percent of his genetic material with humans. The chimpanzees, both gracile and robust, are our closest living relatives in the animal kingdom, but the other great apes, gorillas and orangutans, are also very closely related to us. Chimpanzees, in fact, are more closely related to humans than they are to the gorillas.

waterfalls, nestling against the sparkling waters of an African lake—encouraged the belief that this was, indeed, Eden and that chimpanzees were our near ancestors. Chimpanzees moved to the forefront of popular consciousness, especially in America. At the time only primatologists paid attention to the evidence that robust chimpanzees exhibit some of the behaviors we most dislike in ourselves.

Gorillas, the greatest of the great apes, also benefited from the new attitudes toward apes. Field research found that these alleged "monsters" rarely attacked humans except in self-defense, but the huge silverbacks would die to protect their families. The work of Dian Fossey, whose portraits of individual gorillas were featured in *National Geographic* articles and in the book *Gorillas in the Mist,* promoted a new appreciation of these gentle giants. Jane Goodall's book *In the Shadow of Man* was also very influential.

Orangutans, however, remained elusive. The focus of scientific and popular attention was on the African apes; the only Asian great ape was aptly called "the neglected ape." In the 1960s, Barbara Harrison, wife of Tom Harrison, who was then head of the Sarawak Museum in the northwest of Borneo, published her interesting book, *Orangutan.* Barbara Harrison had rescued and raised orphaned infant orangutans, some of whom entered the first orangutan rehabilitation program for return to the wild. But her encounters with wild orangutans were fleeting. Even the dedicated field biologist George Schaller, who spent months in Sarawak, reported that the red apes were exceedingly difficult to find and study.

When I went into the field in 1971, encouraged by Louis Leakey like Jane Goodall and Dian Fossey before me, knowledge of wild orangutans barely filled a page. Western scientists had just completed a two-year study of orangutans in North Borneo (Sabah) and East Borneo, but the results had not yet been published. When I first arrived in Kalimantan (Indonesian Borneo) the mystery surrounding orangutans was so great that no one knew whether they were social or solitary, herbivorous or fruit-eaters, totally arboreal or semiterrestrial. Now we know that orangutans are semi-solitary, primarily frugivorous or fruit-eaters, occasionally come down to the ground, and at one site, even systematically make tools. We also know that they are on the verge of extinction; estimates put the number of orangutans still in the wild at fewer than 30,000.

Westerners have by now adopted the great apes along with other endangered species as being worthy of respect and protection. Along with whales and pandas, great apes are "charismatic megafauna"—large animals who capture popular imagination and inspire compassion. Millions of people have "seen" great apes face-to-face on increasingly popular television nature programs, and recognized their humanlike qualities. Support organizations have been created to protect our closest relatives. The Great Apes Project, dedicated to treating

LEFT
Six immature robust chimpanzees together, five sitting in a tree and one below, indicates both the gregarious nature of chimpanzees and the fact that they seem equally at ease on the ground and in the trees.

OPPOSITE
Both wild-born, a male and female chimpanzee interact in a tree at a sanctuary in Zambia. The relative ease with which this photo was taken belies the difficulty researchers first had habituating wild chimpanzees to their presence. It took Jane Goodall several years before wild chimpanzees would accept her, while pioneering Japanese primatologists resorted to provisioning (providing food) wild chimpanzees in the Mahale region in order to observe them.

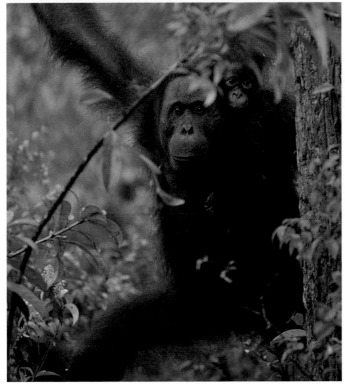

humans and great apes as equals with the same basic rights, and to changing their legal status from that of property to that of persons, has a growing international constituency. In 2001, the United Nations launched the Great Apes Survival Program (GRASP), bringing together wildlife groups and charities from around the world, for urgent action. The ideal of conservation is slowly becoming part of our moral fabric. The days when hunters routinely shot apes and proudly displayed their morbid trophies may be gone as well as the time when scientists ended a field study by killing their subjects and dissecting the corpses. Nevertheless, we are driving the great apes into extinction, not so much out of nineteenth-century egocentrism and bravado, but through ignorance and carelessness. The exploitation of African and Southeast Asian tropical rain forests for timber, mining, and commercial agriculture has all but destroyed the great apes' habitats in a mere two or three generations.

In Africa, countless mining and logging communities depend on the "bushmeat trade," the wholesale slaughter of wild animals without regard to their future survival or that of local people. In Borneo and Sumatra, past and current logging and mining as well as farming and plantations leave thin tropical soil barren, forcing orangutans into a decreasing number of isolated pockets of forest. For many great ape populations, it is already too late. Many populations are already extinct. Only radical action, on the part of private industry and governments as well as conservation groups, will allow a future for great apes in the wild. Otherwise, we will be left alone on the planet with no family to call our own except for ourselves, humans. Our blood kin, the great apes, will remain only as prisoners in our laboratories, zoos, and welfare sanctuaries. As Jane Goodall and others have repeatedly said, out of our understanding of the great apes will come love, and out of that love will come the action that is needed to save them. My fervent hope is that the next chapters of this book will help provide the understanding that will begin the process leading to action.

CHIMPANZEES: OUR SIBLING SPECIES, ROBUST AND GRACILE

Ah, now we must re-define tool, re-define man—or accept chimpanzees as humans!

LOUIS LEAKEY *on Jane Goodall's finding tool use and tool making among the wild chimpanzees at Gombe*

In sum, the place of the human species in the natural order is predicated on the place of the chimpanzee, and is consequently a contested site on the boundary of animalness and godliness, beast and angel.

JONATHAN MARKS

IN SENEGAL AN ANTHROPOLOGIST collecting stories about great apes discovered why some local people refuse to kill or eat chimpanzees. Long ago, a man walking in the forest fell into a hole, probably a hunting trap, and, wounded and hurt, couldn't crawl out. A group of chimpanzees happened by and noticed him. The chimpanzees started calling. They called for so long and so persistently that local people followed the alarm to the middle of the forest, and rescued the man. Grateful to the chimpanzees for helping to save a human life, the local people resolved never to hunt chimpanzees again.

This story, possibly apocryphal, underscores the chimpanzee's status as humankind's sibling, not only in genetic and evolutionary terms, but also in terms of behavior.

For hundreds of years scientists and naturalists have recognized that chimpanzees and humans are very similar. The first anatomical comparisons performed by Tysen in 1699 clearly established our bodily similarities. But not until the late twentieth century did anyone realize just how close we are. In 1975 two geneticists from the University of California at Berkeley, C. King and A. Wilson, went past the anatomical comparisons. A center for the avant-garde, Berkeley has frequently been in the forefront of academic and intellectual trends. Probably for the first time in science, researchers attempted to *quantify* the underlying similarity between humans and great apes. King and Wilson looked at proteins, which reflect gene structure. By comparing proteins, they derived a startling number: chimpanzee and human proteins are 99.3 percent identical. Other studies have indicated that humans share more than 98.3 percent identity with chimpanzees in typical nuclear noncoding DNA sequences. These numbers entered the lexicon of popular Western thought and culture and solidified the view that humans and chimpanzees are sibling species.

The Pulitzer Prize–winning UCLA physiologist Jared Diamond later suggested in his book *The Third Chimpanzee* that humans and chimpanzees are similar enough to warrant classifying them as members of the same genus. There are two recognized chimpanzee species—the robust chimpanzee (once referred to as the "common chimpanzee") and the gracile chimpanzee or bonobo (once called the "pygmy chimpanzee"). The third chimpanzee is humankind.

Most scientists now agree that chimpanzees are our closest living relatives in the animal kingdom. In fact, they are so closely related to us that, once blood types are matched, humans can receive blood from a chimpanzee and vice versa. After a transfusion, both humans and chimpanzees develop antibodies to the blood so the transfusion cannot be carried out a second time. Significantly, humans cannot exchange blood with gorillas or orangutans. Neither can chimpanzees donate blood to the other great apes.

Ironically, while some scientists and others might agree that humans are another type of chimpanzee, most shy away from calling chimpanzees human. Whatever they are, chimpanzees are very much like people, sometimes almost frighteningly so. It's not just their blood, their proteins, and their general anatomy but also their emotions, high cognitive abilities, and behavior that make them so similar to us. A number of scientists who have studied chimpanzees in the wild would argue that chimpanzees should be treated as humankind's moral equivalent. A number of philosophers and scientists have endorsed the Great Apes Project, which calls for chimpanzees and the other great apes to be granted the same rights to "life, liberty, and the pursuit of happiness" that human beings enjoy. Certainly, chimpanzees are endlessly fascinating to people. Indeed, many children's books feature chimpanzee or chimpanzee-like characters, such as my own childhood favorite, *Curious George*. They seem so much like us but are not us. It is the endless paradox of our fascination with the chimpanzee.

Here, at a sanctuary in Kenya, chimpanzee youngsters keep their cultural traditions alive by attempting to fish for termites with plant stems. Perhaps not as practiced or as successful as experienced wild adult chimpanzees, one youngster uses his finger to probe the termite mound while his stem tool sits in his other hand. Termite fishing is not as easy as it looks. Geza Teleki, now a distinguished conservationist, but once a young graduate student at Gombe, tried to fish for termites. He concluded, after many attempts, that he simply wasn't as good at it as young chimpanzees, never mind adults.

LEFT

A female chimpanzee checks out the stiff apparatus of a male chimpanzee. Chimpanzee males have very large testes compared to the other great apes, indicating greater competition among the males for sexual access to females. A male will sometimes try to take a female "on safari" to the borders of the community's territory so that he can monopolize her sexually while she is receptive. Females may resist, as the periphery is dangerous: the consorting pair could easily encounter aggressive neighbors on patrol.

TOP

Orphaned youngsters interact in the safety of a sanctuary. One youngster is suckling the lower lip of another, possibly as a substitute for his dead mother's nipple. In captivity, an infant's urgent need to suckle often will not be denied, despite the lack of milk.

BOTTOM

At a sanctuary in Zambia, a young adult male chimpanzee examines the large posterior pink swelling of a female, a sure sign that she is ovulating. While these large female swellings are typical of chimpanzees, they are not in gorillas or orangutans.

To the trained observer all chimpanzees are not alike. Originally, chimpanzees were divided into a dozen or more species, but in recent years only two species have been recognized: *Pan troglodytes* or "common chimpanzees," more correctly called robust chimpanzees, and *Pan paniscus* or bonobos (identified as a distinct species only in 1933) and originally called "pygmy chimpanzees," now also called gracile chimpanzees.

A recent classification divides common chimpanzees into four subspecies: *verus*, the West African, or pale-faced or masked chimpanzee; the Nigerian *vellerosus*; the central African *troglodytes* or black-faced chimpanzee; and finally, the east African *schweinfurthi* or eastern long-haired chimpanzee. These four subspecies and the gracile chimpanzee occupy mutually exclusive geographical areas.

Genetic analysis suggests that most chimpanzees in laboratories or zoos in North America originated from West Africa with very few from Nigeria or East Africa. Yet, the most famous wild chimpanzees, those Jane Goodall and Toshida Nishida studied in Gombe and Mahale, both in Tanzania, belong to the eastern long-haired chimpanzee. Perhaps someday taxonomists will raise these populations to separate species status but, for now, they look secure as subspecies. Indeed, in captivity chimpanzees from different populations have mated and produced offspring.

There are tales of another subspecies of chimpanzee called the koolo-kamba, said to live in the southern Sudan. My late colleague Dian Fossey, who studied mountain gorillas, was fascinated by descriptions of these creatures and always hoped one day to "check them out." The koolo-kamba are said to be a cross between gorillas and chimpanzees. These creatures are reputed to be absolutely black with thick hair (like a mountain gorilla) and large feet. Most scientists dismiss them as a myth but their story lingers. Perhaps these chimpanzees are a variant of the central African black-faced chimpanzee subspecies. Nobody knows. And Dian, unfortunately, didn't live long enough to find out.

Fifty years ago chimpanzees ranged through 25 countries in a wide belt across equatorial Africa from Senegal to Tanzania. Their ranges included, among other countries, Sierra Leone, Guinea, Cameroon, Gabon, Congo, Democratic Republic of the Congo (DRC), Nigeria, and Uganda. There were probably hundreds of thousands of these so-called common chimpanzees back then, but in recent years their numbers have declined rapidly and "common" no longer applies! It is better to call them robust chimpanzees.

Although bonobos are undoubtedly chimpanzees, the people who study them rarely call them just chimpanzees, preferring the term bonobo or gracile chimpanzee. I always assumed that *bonobo* was the word for these animals in a native African language or dialect. Much to my surprise, I was told it wasn't so. "Bolobo" is the name of the village in Africa from which a group of these primates was shipped to Europe

sometime in the mid-twentieth century. The crates were labeled "Bonobo," which was a misspelling of the village's name. Transferred to the animals, the name slowly caught on, especially among people who knew that the old term pygmy chimpanzee was a misnomer.

Neither are bonobos merely smaller versions of robust chimpanzees. Initially only bonobo skins and skeletons were studied, rather than the live animals themselves, which might have given rise to the pygmy idea. Bonobos could be called the supermodels of the chimpanzee world, for they are more gracile, or slender, than other chimpanzees and have longer legs, smaller heads, and flatter faces. Their teeth are also smaller. For unknown reasons, they frequently have webbing between the second and third toe. While robust chimpanzees are born with whitish pink faces, bonobos have black faces. Bonobos also tend to be blacker than other chimpanzees and sometimes are less hairy. Adults occasionally sport curious tufts of hair on each side of their heads, reminiscent of balding medieval monks.

Robust chimpanzees, on the other hand, have black body hair (although very rare, ginger-colored individuals have been spotted in the wild), short white beards, and prominent ears. Infants are born with pink faces, which change to black or brown in adulthood, and a conspicuous tuft of white hair on their rear end, which marks them as "infants." As individuals age, they sometimes develop gray backs. Their skin color is usually light, almost white, except for their hands, feet, and face, which are black.

Robust chimpanzees are powerfully built and, like bonobos, have long arms and short, somewhat bowed legs. Chimpanzees cannot lock their knees and so are not the most efficient bipedal walkers. They are long-distance quadrupedal knuckle-walkers with the hands and wrists of their front limbs supporting most of the body's weight as they move along the ground, sometimes surprisingly rapidly. Hugo van Lawick, Jane Goodall's first husband and the brilliant photographer and cinematographer who documented her work, once told me that racing uphill he had been able to outrun robust chimpanzees but just barely. Apparently, the runners, both chimpanzee and human, are evenly matched.

Chimpanzees, robust and gracile, are also very much at ease in the trees, skillfully climbing, leaping, and brachiating in the canopy as well as sitting on, and hanging from branches. They are quite versatile creatures and can occupy a variety of habitats and terrains, except water: we humans swim but chimpanzees don't, at least not in the wild.

It goes without saying that the behavior of chimpanzees and the other great apes has always been of intense interest to scientists, especially those concerned with human evolution. This is why the great paleoanthropologist Louis Leakey had sought out and encouraged scientists such as Jane Goodall,

Dian Fossey, and myself (collectively called the three angels or the trimates) to study the great apes in the wild. Since chimpanzees are the "gold standard" against which human uniqueness is judged, it is not surprising, that they are among the most thoroughly studied animals in the world. This is despite the fact that they generally live in inhospitable and inaccessible places, far from the traditional routes of commerce and travel, and are extremely shy and wary of observers, as well as being wide ranging animals difficult to track.

Jane Goodall was not the first to study chimpanzees scientifically. But, with the support of Louis Leakey, she initiated the first long-term and longest-running field study of wild chimpanzees at what is now called Gombe National Park, formerly Gombe Stream Reserve, in Tanzania. Her observations at Gombe of wild chimpanzees using and manufacturing tools, hunting other animals and eating and sharing meat, forever changed the way we view ourselves and our place in nature. Jane Goodall's observations were a revelation. They demonstrated that we humans are not as unique among primates or among animals as we once thought we were. Although not as well known to the general public, the chimpanzee studies of Toshida Nishida, Jun'ichiro Itani, Kinji Imunishi, Y. Sugiyama, Tetsuro Matsuzawa, and others from Kyoto University, Japan, also deeply influenced how we humans define ourselves. The results of their studies also emphasized how chimpanzee behavior very much parallels our own. In particular, Japanese scientists Itani and Nishida provided us with a comprehensive understanding of chimpanzee sociability and social system.

The Japanese scientists from Kyoto University and Jane Goodall independently began their pioneering chimpanzee studies almost half a century ago. Both Imanishi and Itani are deceased now while Nishida recently retired. The indefatigable Jane Goodall continues her work but, given the calamitous situation facing wild chimpanzees, she devotes most of her attention today to conservation of and protection of chimpanzees, including captive and laboratory chimpanzees.

The study of chimpanzees in West Africa started much later than in East Africa. The first long-term study there was carried out by Yukimaru Sugiyama at Bossou near the Nimba Mountains in Guinea. Sugiyama and his local collaborators reported in 1979 that the chimpanzees at Bossou used a pair of stones like a hammer and anvil to crack open oil palm nuts to obtain the edible kernel inside the hard shell. This was the first report of wild chimpanzees using stone tools for feeding. Since such stone tool use was unknown among the chimpanzees of East Africa, this was the first glimmer that there was a wide diversity in the cultural traditions of different chimpanzee populations throughout Africa.

Today there are at least five main sites where long-term studies of wild chimpanzees in Africa are carried out. Gombe

An adolescent male chimpanzee at a sanctuary in Kenya looks out from the trees. There are no wild chimpanzees in Kenya. His mother was killed in a neighboring country, probably for the bushmeat trade. The large ears are typical of chimpanzees.

National Park and Mahale National Park in Tanzania are the best known. Other studies are in Kibale National Park, Uganda, directed by researchers from Harvard; Tai Forest National Park in Côte d'Ivoire headed by C. Boesch; and Bossou in Guinea. Bossou has the longest history of any wild chimpanzee site in West Africa and, along with Mahale, symbolizes the rich collaboration between African and Japanese researchers that has characterized wild chimpanzee studies.

Wild chimpanzees are complicated creatures living rich and complex lives. Debate about wild robust chimpanzee social organization has continued for years. In the early 1960s, A. Kortlandt described temporary associations of up to 30 individuals among the wild chimpanzees he studied in the (then) Belgian Congo, now DRC. Some groups contained both males and females; others consisted of females and their young, so-called nursery groups. However, British scientists Goodall and Vernon F. Reynolds independently described robust chimpanzees as living in "open" societies, meaning that individuals could associate with whomever they pleased and that community boundaries were open to newcomers. In other words, the stranger was welcome.

The Goodall/Reynolds description was particularly seductive because it coincided with the youth culture of the mid-sixties, which held that humans were intuitively cooperative and peaceful ("make love, not war"). It also suggested that the story of human evolution paralleled the Biblical story of humankind's expulsion from Eden. If, indeed, chimpanzees were almost-ancestors, a reflection of Eden, then, of course, they should be gentle vegetarians thriving in peaceful, open communities. Even after Jane Goodall discovered that robust chimpanzees hunt and eat meat, exploding the vegetarian myth, the idyllic image of chimpanzees lingered. Goodall's finding that chimpanzees make and use tools, long thought to be uniquely human activities, attracted more attention. This challenge to our sense of human superiority caused excitement in the general public as well as among evolutionary scientists, in large part because of Goodall herself.

The story was told over and over again in television specials, magazines, and books featuring the graceful image of a slim attractive blonde in khaki shorts, beautiful and smart enough to play herself in the Hollywood movie if ever one was made. When I was a teaching assistant in the Department of Anthropology at UCLA, just before I went to Indonesia for the first time, I showed Hugo van Lawick's films of Jane and the Gombe chimpanzees to my classes. One young man told me that the first time he watched the films, it was to see the chimpanzees, but then he came back a second time to see Jane Goodall!

Perhaps Nishida and his Japanese colleagues never watched the National Geographic specials. On the basis of his long-term studies in the Mahale Mountains south of Gombe, Nishida

established the stable semiclosed nature of wild chimpanzee communities. While males generally spend their entire lives living in their natal communities, females occasionally transfer to neighboring communities during adolescence, sometimes coming back home, sometimes not. This is the prevailing view of robust chimpanzee social organization held today. The picture seems to hold, with some variation, over the entire range of robust chimpanzee populations. As far as males and older females are concerned, robust chimpanzees definitely do not live in open societies!

Once again, it was Jane Goodall and her colleagues who documented territoriality in chimpanzee communities. In fact, robust chimpanzees are probably unique among primates (other than humans themselves) in that they commonly engage in lethal aggression involving coalitions of group members against other communities. Direct contact between communities is usually hostile. The hostility is so severe that it may result in brutal beatings and death. Indeed, Goodall and her associates documented the extermination of one community, the Kahama, at the hands (and teeth) of an adjacent group. The two communities had shared an era of peace in the time of abundant resources. Unfortunately, it was the bananas the researchers provided at daily feedings that created a false sense of plenty. Once the plenty ended, the fragile peace ended as well. A similar extermination probably occurred at Mahale but was not so well documented.

The violence among communities is primarily a male activity, although adult females occasionally participate as well. Patrolling seems to be a basic element of chimpanzee territoriality. At various locales and sites, patrols occur regularly, once to three times per month. Behavior changes radically during patrols. Normally, male chimpanzees are loud and conspicuous, generally preferring the center of community range. The patrolling males are silent and seemingly very wary, moving quietly in single file, often stopping to scan their surroundings, to listen, and to sniff the ground. Males show an extraordinary heightened interest in the evidence of other chimpanzees' past presence in the vicinity, not only inspecting old ground nests and feces, but also even dropped food remains. On patrol they form parties that not only travel along the edges of community territory, but also make deep incursions, sometimes almost a mile, into the territories of neighboring communities.

Presumably, the goal of these patrols is to "keep tabs" on the neighbors. Yet patrolling chimpanzees do not always contact members of other communities, either directly or vocally. In about half of the patrols observed, male chimpanzees approached, chased, or attacked members of the other group; in the other half they either avoided contact or fled. Why? The reason is simple. Large groups who outnumber their neighboring group are aggressive and loud, while patrol parties from smaller groups tend to avoid or flee

from encounters. In fact, when adult male members are reduced to three or less in a community, they change their tactics. Rather than patrolling for neighbors, these males switch to avoiding all contact.

At the end, the Kahama community of chimpanzees at Gombe was reduced to three adult males, who traveled everywhere together, always wary and alert. The grief-stricken researcher who last observed them said she felt that they understood the danger posed by the Kasakala males, who had murdered many of their relatives and community members. Ironically, by demolishing the Kahama community, the Kasakala males removed a buffer between themselves and a larger, more vigorous community. The Kasakala males were, in turn, themselves hunted down and beaten by males from this larger community. For a while it looked as though Kasakala would be eliminated. But after some years, as young males became adult and joined the battle, the community recovered.

What benefit do robust chimpanzee communities receive by patrolling and attacking members of other communities to the point of extermination? Theoretically, the benefits are many and the hypotheses proposed to explain territorial behavior numerous. Such benefits may include better access to resources, particularly food, and, for the males, sexual access to more females, as well as better security for all community members. Interestingly, one study indicated that male chimpanzee participation in patrols correlated with that "holy grail" of all nature: reproductive success. The aggressive males who most actively patrolled seemed to be the ones who most frequently mated.

It's not surprising that most females with offspring do not participate. Patrolling individuals face brutal attacks, injury, and even death. Attacking male chimpanzees will kill females' infants and even cannibalize them. This is extraordinarily rare behavior for a primate (with the possible exception of humans). In the Indian subcontinent hanuman langur males sometimes kill infants when the male monkeys enter new troops, but they generally do not eat their small victims. Unlike infanticide by male primates documented in other species, where cannibalism does not occur, this robust chimpanzee behavior does not seem to revolve around male reproductive success. Chimpanzee males don't seem to be recruiting neighboring females with these extreme tactics. Rather they seem to be attempting to intimidate the females and, through them, delivering threatening messages to the males of the neighboring community. They seem to be saying, This is who we are and this is what we are capable of doing. It is behavior remarkably similar to our own. Since robust chimpanzees are our close relatives, some scientists and writers argue that "demonic males" are part of our own evolutionary legacy and are to be expected in the human species as well. Aggression, war, territorial behavior, infanticide, and cannibalism exist in the males of our own species

In the Mahale Mountains, a wild chimpanzee enjoys a wild lemon. Although they are primarily fruit-eaters, some scientists have called chimpanzees omnivorous because of the wide range of foods they eat, including, at some sites, the meat of other mammals such as young red colobus monkeys, which they sometimes kill, share with others, and devour. Chimpanzees also fish termites out of mounds with prepared sticks that they sometimes actually carry from one mound to the next.

because these are the behaviors that have led to success for males—or so the argument goes.

Forgotten in the argument for "natural male aggression" is the existence of another chimpanzee species, equally related to us. Unfortunately, this gracile chimpanzee, the bonobo, lives in the impenetrable heart of Africa, deep in the Congo forest. War and difficult terrain have made the bonobo extremely difficult to study. Louis Leakey died before he could send out a fourth angel to study these chimpanzees. In fact, when my orangutan study had seemed hopeless, he turned to me and said, "So it will be pygmy chimpanzees then?" I refused to abandon my quest for an orangutan study. A year later, just before I left for Indonesia, Louis told me that he had just found her, the one that he would support for long-term bonobo studies. I regret that his potential fourth angel's study of bonobos was halted by his death. Who knows what we might now understand about gracile chimpanzees if this angel's long-term study had materialized?

Genetically, robust and gracile chimpanzees are equally related to humans, but it is the better-known robust chimpanzees that are routinely used as the model for our common ancestors. However, some scientists have long suspected that the gracile chimpanzees resemble our ancestors more than any other creature. When Adrienne Zihlman and her co-workers found that the long-legged, gracile chimpanzees most resemble the australopithecines, this suspicion was upheld. But other scientists have argued that our ancestors' morphological patterns were more similar to the robust chimpanzee. It is generally believed that bonobos by themselves are not our closest living relatives in the animal kingdom. They share that honor, if you will, with the robust chimpanzees. The split between the robust and gracile chimpanzees occurred millions of years *after* ancestral chimpanzees split off from the ancestors of humans. Humankind is equally related, evolutionarily and genetically, to both species of chimpanzee. And, therefore, both chimpanzees may be equally relevant to an understanding of our place, as humans, on this earth.

The gracile chimpanzees are as different in their behavior from the robust chimpanzees as it is possible to be, and yet remain a chimpanzee, belying the notion that genetic identity can be used to extrapolate most characteristics shared by humans and their ancestor. It can't. Robust chimpanzees support certain ideas about human origins and inborn human behavior developed over the past half century, concepts emphasizing aggressiveness, dominance, male bonding, and war. The popular literature about human origins is filled with titles such as *The Territorial Animal* and *Killer-Ape*. The emphasis is not on humankind, but on how the territoriality and aggressive behavior of men has shaped human evolution. One of my texts in college was *Man, the Tool-user*. According to this scenario, the stone tools men used in hunting and butcher-

OPPOSITE

A wild chimpanzee mother and her infant sit on the forest floor at Gombe National Park, Tanzania. Even in the complex society of the territorial chimpanzee, the most enduring social bond is between a mother and her adult daughter.

TOP

A trio of orphaned infant chimpanzees at Chimfunshi Sanctuary in Zambia lean on each other to survive the brutal traumas that brought them here. But they are the lucky ones. Most infants whose mothers are killed end up dead or in the pet trade, soon to die.

BOTTOM

A wild chimpanzee mother and her dependent youngster stare out of the forest in Mahale, Tanzania. Chimpanzees live in communities consisting of related males defending a communal territory. Typically, only females transfer from one community to another.

ing fuelled human evolution. Robust chimpanzees support this position. Robust chimpanzees, like men, are from Mars.

The concept of humans as killer apes has a long pedigree, perhaps springing from the story of Cain and Abel. Raymond Dart gave this concept new life in 1925. When he found a juvenile hominid skull in a box of gravel, he proposed a new species *Australopithecus africanus,* the earliest bipedal hominid known at that time. Dart held that *Australopithecus* was an aggressive tool-using carnivore. Robert Ardrey and Nobel Prize–winner Konrad Lorenz dramatized and augmented these ideas in their popular writings. They argued that aggression and hunting promoted male bonding, which in turn, drove the development of tools and cultural progress.

These were bold ideas supported by the evidence at the time. But "spoilsport" scientists and others demonstrated that aggression can be learned and that some human cultures seem remarkably peaceful. Some social scientists pointed to the chimpanzees, who were thought to be peaceful vegetarians in the Edens of Gombe and Budongo. Then, through Jane Goodall's research and observations, the entire edifice of the peaceful vegetarian chimpanzee collapsed, strengthening the "killer ape" hypothesis. Since then some authors have returned to the "killer ape" scenarios in books that attempt to demonstrate that chimpanzee and human males are exceptionally violent. In *Demonic Males*, the authors, Richard Wrangham and Dale Peterson, have even included gorillas and orangutans. They conclude that since robust chimpanzees are "surprisingly excellent models of our direct ancestors," chimpanzee-like "violence preceded and paved the way for human war."

But the other chimpanzee, the gentle bonobo, is not from Mars, she is from Venus (and that includes the males of the species as well). Only in the last decade have we learned much about the bonobo. The scientists who brought the gracile chimpanzees to world attention studied them primarily in captivity, not the wild. Sue Savage-Rumbaugh demonstrated their remarkable cognitive and symbolic capabilities, while Frans de Wahl brought attention to their distinct adaptations by drawing on his own captive studies and relating his findings to the studies of other scientists who have worked with gracile chimpanzees in the wild.

In the past, many people assumed that free-ranging chimpanzees preferred not to get their feet wet. Here, a group of orphans wade in the river surrounding their island sanctuary in Congo Brazzaville.

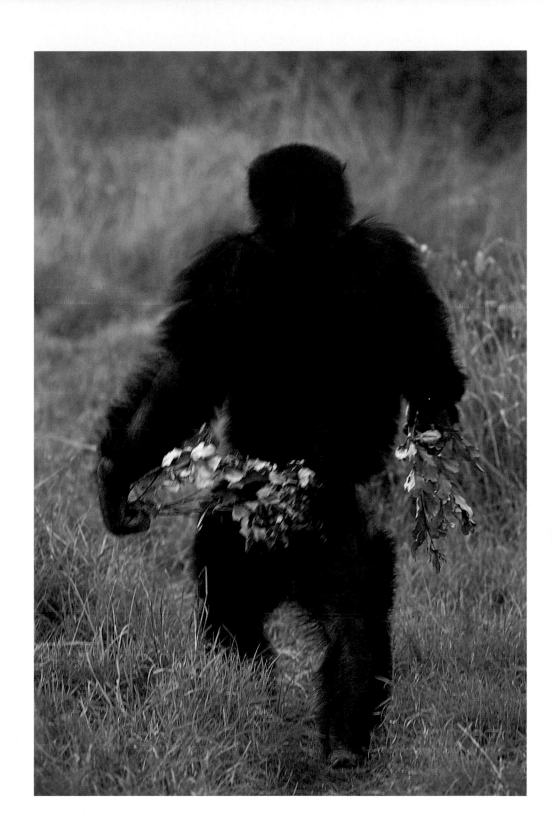

Excellent tool users, chimpanzees have developed skills with tools and tool-making behavioral complexes that are superior among the apes. A chimpanzee youngster at a sanctuary in Kenya uses a stick as part of his display. The ability to hold an erect posture is one of the characteristics that distinguish apes from monkeys.

As part of his display, an adult male chimpanzee at a sanctuary in Kenya runs bipedally while holding twigs in his hands. Such displays tend to be very loud, and when adult males display, the other chimpanzees scatter. Early investigators heard chimpanzees in the forest but rarely actually saw them.

The bonobo was not studied in the wild until well into the 1970s, and the first major publications on wild populations date from the early 1980s. One reason is their range in the Congo River Basin. Studying bonobos in the wild is difficult, in part due to the dense terrain that bonobos inhabit, in part because of the civil unrest that constantly plagues the region. Joseph Conrad's book *Heart of Darkness* is about the darkness in the heart of the Congo River Basin. That basin is dark, dank, and sinister, not only in its steamy vegetation, but primarily in its brutal colonial history and bloody aftermath.

When bonobo social organization was finally understood, it was a revelation. There are no intercommunity patrols, no attacks and deaths on the territorial boundary, no infanticide, no cooperative hunting, no male coalitions terrorizing the group, and not much evidence of the lethal aggression that seemingly characterizes robust chimpanzees.

LEFT
Full speed ahead! At a sanctuary in Kenya a chimpanzee runs using the quadrupedal knuckle-walking locomotion typical of African apes on the ground.

OPPOSITE
A bonobo youngster swings on a liana. The increased availability of guns among Africans combined with the breakdown of traditional culture, fueled by ever persistent civil war in DRC, has exponentially increased the bushmeat trade, bringing larger numbers of orphans to sanctuaries such as this one.

But unlike the classic pronouncements of Jane Goodall on robust chimpanzees, these announcements were not made as press releases to the mass media. People already knew about chimpanzees, or thought they did. Reports of the "other chimpanzee" seemed like an afterthought. Who knows? Had gracile chimpanzees been studied before the robust, perhaps our view of human heritage would be different.

Sex, not war or aggression, pervades all aspects of the gracile chimpanzee's life. Sex, not grooming, is the lubricant that facilitates all social interaction. Not only is male-female sex common but so is male-male, female-female, female-juvenile and male-juvenile. Sexual activity is omnipresent. Particularly common among adult female bonobos is genito-genital rubbing, also called GG-rubbing. Totally unknown among robust chimpanzees (and gorillas and orangutans as well), this behavior is found among every bonobo group ever observed for any length of time, whether in the wild or in captivity. It is probably the most distinctive behavior of the bonobos. One female stands on hands and feet; another female clasps her arms and legs around the first female, clinging to her underside; then the first female lifts the other off the ground. The two females rub their genital swellings together rhythmically as if they were copulating with a male. Bonobo females have large prominent clitorises. As to whether GG-rubbing results in orgasm, their grins and squeals certainly suggest that something pleasurable is occurring. Male bonobos have their own version of GG-rubbing. They stand back to back and rub their large scrotums together.

The amount and variety of bonobo sex is astounding. They do it all: oral sex, French-kissing, manual manipulation of one another's genitalia, and so on. Masturbation is minimal compared to the social sex. Frans de Waal documented that, in captivity, gracile chimpanzees not only engage in ten times more sexual activity than robust chimpanzees but also demonstrate astonishing variety in the forms this activity takes compared to the robust chimpanzees. He made the astute observation that film or television crews shooting popular programs frequently turn their cameras off when bonobos are sexually active. Even today! Thus, much of bonobo behavior isn't recorded. In contrast, fighting, hunting, and other violent behavior found among robust chimpanzees is always recorded when camera crews are present, perhaps exaggerating the frequency of its occurrence in comparison with sex in bonobos.

I've had my own experiences with chimpanzees, both robust and gracile. The first time I met bonobos was on a visit with Sue Savage-Rumbaugh at Yerkes Primate Center in Georgia. It was a beautiful crisp day with the sun shining. To get to the bonobos I had to walk past cages full of robust chimpanzees, who as I approached them went beserk. I walked a gauntlet of loud vocalizations and vigorous acrobatics. Yet when I reached the bonobos, they were utterly silent. Sue motioned

OPPOSITE
A female bonobo gazes into the distance. Her relative lack of body hair is unusual for chimpanzees, whether robust or gracile, and is perhaps a response to nutritional or emotional stress.

RIGHT
An adolescent bonobo checks out fingers with a lip. All great apes use their mouth as a fifth hand.

me to whisper so as to not disturb them. I was allowed to go right up to the wire fence and squat next to it. After a short while, an adult bonobo male quietly came up and made a small slapping motion in my direction. He clearly didn't appreciate my presence close to his family, which included mothers and immatures, so I immediately moved away. The noise of the robust chimpanzees still booming in the distance only served to emphasize the bonobos' silence.

My next interaction with bonobos occurred many years later at the Columbus Zoo, in Ohio. I had what I suppose could be called the equivalent of telephone sex with an adolescent male bonobo behind cage bars. His eyes fastened on mine, and he vocalized intensely as he moved rhythmically against the bars. His intensity and vocalizations drew me into his experience and I found myself moved as I stood watching him from a distance.

Somewhat like robust chimpanzees, gracile chimpanzees live in communities consisting of related males and unrelated females. Female adolescents leave their birth community when they first develop small sexual swellings. Adolescent females visit different neighboring communities as transients, eventually settling down permanently in one community. During this transition, bonobo female sexuality blooms. Suddenly adolescent females are copulating with strange males and GG-rubbing with older females in distant forests far away from their known kin. Their swellings grow larger continuously until finally at about ten years of age they reach full size. At about thirteen or fourteen years of age the female gives birth to her first infant. By this time she has integrated herself into her new community. She does so by attaching herself to one or two older females and by initiating grooming and sexual activity. Gradually, over the years, as she has more offspring and becomes older and more senior, young migrating females seek her presence as they themselves move into the community. This entire process is facilitated by the high sociability and sexuality of bonobo females. Females like each other's company. They seek each other out, behavior that is not necessarily seen among the other African apes. They follow one another, groom, and GG-rub together. Despite the fact that females are not related and males are, bonobo communities are female-bonded.

Males stay in their natal community, remaining attached to their mothers all their lives. Males compete intensely for dominance but, unlike the robust chimpanzees, they depend on their mother's active support. Males whose mothers have died or are feeble due to age tend to lose their dominance. Among the robust chimpanzees, mother's rank clearly has some influence; at Gombe dominant female Flo's son Figan, supported by older brother Faben, became alpha. But the mother's direct intervention was not important. The battles and conflicts were waged almost entirely without Flo's direct intervention. It was Faben's support that was probably crucial for his younger brother's ascent to dominance. Interestingly, bonobo males focus on their

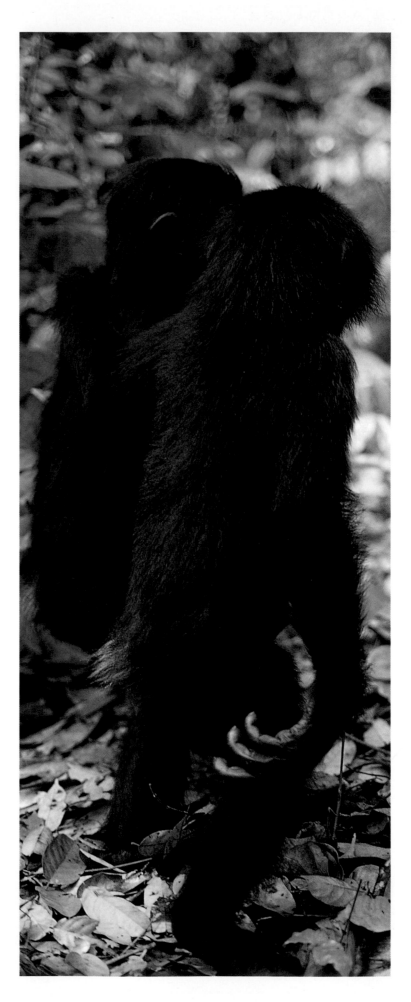

LEFT
Two orphaned bonobos have become attached to one another at a sanctuary in DRC. In the wild, infants such as these would each be carried by their mothers and would have almost continuous tactile contact with her for the first year of life. Out of necessity, these young orphans have come to rely on each other.

OPPOSITE
An old wild male bonobo with fingers missing as a result of fights with other bonobos, probably males, illustrates that living in a sexually oriented society dominated by females still has its aggravations. He also seems to be blind in one eye.

mother, not their brothers. Male alliances, even among brothers, are de-emphasized. Takayoshi Kano, one of the Japanese fieldworkers who pioneered bonobo research in the wild, called mothers the core of bonobo society. Unlike gracile chimpanzees, robust chimpanzee males are almost totally dominant over females in the wild, where young adult robust chimpanzees first climb the adult female hierarchy and, having defeated all the females, begin their ascent up the male hierarchy. The lowest ranking adult male is always higher than the most dominant female.

But among bonobos, females *collectively* dominate males. They do so by associating together, forming coalitions, and dominating their sons. Females dominate even to the point of taking prized foods from males. Kano stressed that males frequently behave submissively to dominant females. But females being females, the bonobo female hierarchy, based on residency and seniority, is relatively loose. Conflict and aggression in bonobo society (and it does occur, particularly in the dominance squabbles of the males) is frequently resolved by sexual contact.

What accounts for this difference between Mars and Venus? At least in part, the basic differences between robust and gracile chimpanzees can be explained by differences in their ecologies. Both species are ripe fruit-eaters, but the fruit trees utilized by bonobos generally are larger than those found in robust chimpanzee ranges, thus there is less competition for food. This also allows bonobo females to congregate in larger groups when feeding. But the trees may be only part of the story. Another part of the explanation, as first pointed out by Richard Wrangham, is the absence of gorillas in bonobo ranges. In most of the robust chimpanzee ranges, gorillas are sympatric. The gorilla's staple foods consist of abundant herbaceous ground vegetation. Robust chimpanzees do not compete well with gorillas for the leafy greens of ground vegetation because gorillas are the ground vegetation specialists. Robust chimpanzees retain their fruit specialization and concentrate on fruit, as well as exploit other food sources such as termites and meat.

But bonobos were freed from competition with gorillas because gorillas were not there. So, in addition to fruit, bonobos have access to additional food, the large quantities of ground vegetation denied robust chimpanzees because it is consumed by gorillas. It's similar (but not identical) to the situation at Gombe when bananas provided by scientists led to a scenario where robust chimpanzees found themselves in a temporary time of plenty. Party sizes grew larger and there were more intense social interactions. Fighting among individuals increased (they are robust chimpanzees after all), but interactions between the two communities attending the banana feedings remained cordial. Eventually the scientists decided to drop the banana provisioning. The consequences for the chimpanzees were disastrous. The peace was broken and one

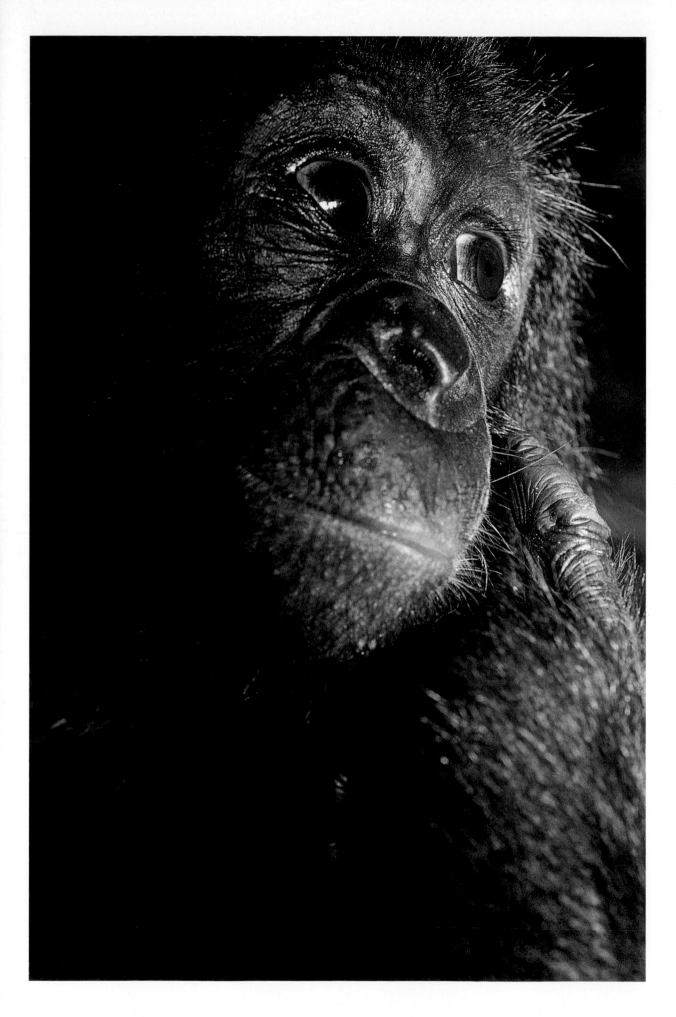

LEFT

An orphan bonobo at a
sanctuary in DRC has an
almost wistful gaze. Of all
the African apes, bonobos,
restricted to one country
that has long been con-
vulsed by civil war, face
the most uncertain future.

OPPOSITE

Sitting in one of the few
North American zoos that
house bonobos, this one
displays the tufts of hair
on both sides of the head
that are characteristic
of bonobos.

community annihilated the other. For the bonobos, the time of plenty is permanent and they have had ample time to evolve into it. Bonobos feed together in large parties because they have access to additional sources of food, the large quantities of leafy greens denied robust chimpanzees. This food occurs in large concentrations and bonobos can feed in large gregarious parties. Over the millennia bonobo sociality and bonding have strengthened as the permanent plenty of food allowed for a permanent peace.

Although aggression does sometimes occur between bonobo communities, it is rare. Interactions among individuals of different communities tend to be peaceful and benign, with much mingling. There is no territorial warfare, no infanticide, no cannibalism, and no lethal violence. While males fight among themselves for a dominant place in the hierarchy, the female hierarchy is loose and relatively relaxed. In contrast to robust chimpanzees, male gracile chimpanzees do not seek alliances among themselves, presumably because the benefits are not worth the trouble. There is no reason for a bonobo to team up with another male to guard a female when sexually eager females are available everywhere. Sexual activity of all sorts cements males and females together in large aggregations. Sexuality also obscures paternity. If everyone is happily mating with everyone else, nobody is sure who the father is. Thus, infanticide has no point: You could end up killing your own offspring—in evolutionary terms, a bad move. Inbreeding is not much of a problem because the females come from outside the community. But maintaining alliances does have its costs; coalitions can be politically difficult and challenging. For bonobo males, it's just easier to have sex.

In addition, coalitions among males do not make sense in a species where females are dominant. The higher the status of females, the greater advantage a male gathers in eschewing coalitions with other males, his sexual competitors, and depending on his mother, with whom there is no sexual competition. As female dominance rises in the species, reliance on good ol' dependable mother becomes increasingly advantageous, as it undermines any latent tendencies to form coalitions among males.

In the end, as we examine chimpanzees we are left with a question: If you were a chimpanzee, and you had the two

Completely absorbed in their own soundmaking, bonobos vocalize at a sanctuary in DRC. The act of holding hands is typical of chimpanzees. Bonobos in particular use touch and sex to defuse potentially violent situations.

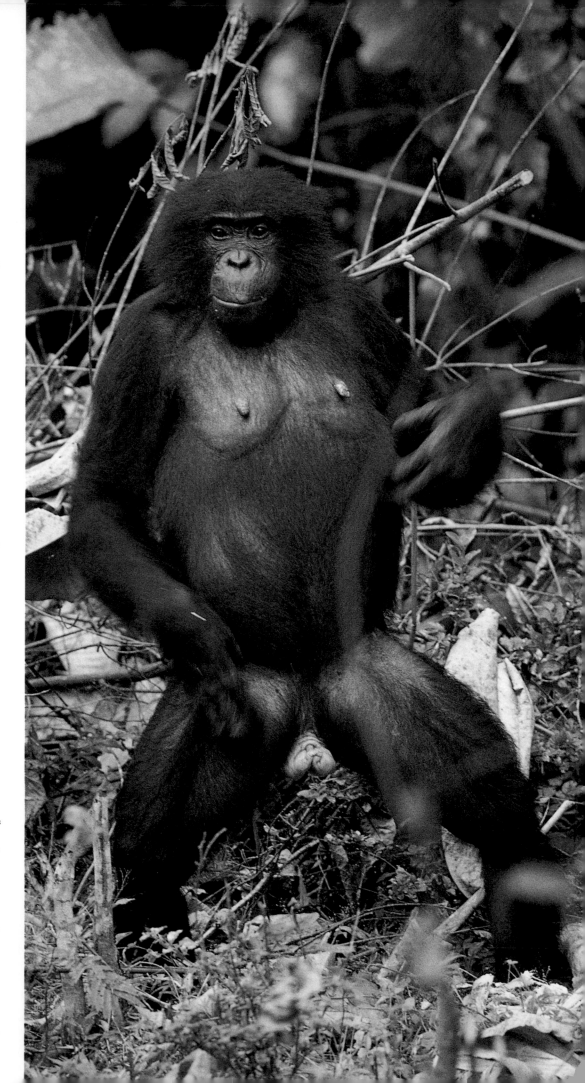

choices available, and ecology and fate didn't dictate the answer, which would you choose? To live in a world run by males or by females? Mars or Venus? In human societies, we have been forced toward Mars. Even in horticultural societies where women own the crop and divorce their husband simply by leaving his sandals outside the dwelling, it is still the men who go to war and defend the group against other groups of men, and men who organize much of the political life of the community. Some people believe that the Neolithic goddess figurines of early Europe, excavated by Marija Gimbutas and her colleagues, are evidence that matriarchal, peaceful, almost bonobo-like horticultural societies existed at one time in central Europe before they were destroyed by chariot-riding and oxen driving patriarchal Indo-Europeans appearing from the East. According to some descriptions of these ancient European societies, women ruled and men concurred. However, this is still in the arena of conjecture. We don't know what these societies were really like.

But the possibility remains that, in the vast diversity of human experience, there were societies different from the ones on this earth today. Both species of chimpanzees can teach us something about humankind and we should study them both equally well. (And examine the conditions that determine the differences in behavior and ecology.) Neither are human but both can help provide answers to questions we care to pose about ourselves. My question is this: If you were a chimpanzee or an ancestral human, which society would you choose as your own? The society run by robust chimpanzee males? Or the society run by bonobo females?

NEAR RIGHT
A wild female bonobo stands looking at the camera at a feeding site at Wamba, DRC. Provisioning was one way used to habituate the wary bonobos to the presence of scientific observers.

OPPOSITE
Face-to-face mating attempts like that taking place between these two orphaned bonobos are typical in the species.

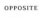

OPPOSITE
Sticks seem to be a favorite
tool among the great apes.
A young upright bonobo at
a sanctuary displays using a
stout stick.

ABOVE
Bonobo orphans vocalize
while holding hands at a
sanctuary. Thanks to the
sanctuary, these bonobos
have a future, though it
will not be in the wild.

RIGHT
When feeding, bonobos
reveal characteristics that
have long led some to
believe them to be evolu-
tionarily closer to humans.
However, although they
have very different social
behaviors, both gracile
and robust chimpanzees
are equally related to
humans genetically.

GORILLAS: GREATEST OF THE APES

From the point of view of hemoglobin structure, it appears that the gorilla is just an abnormal human or man an abnormal gorilla . . .

EMILE ZUCKERKANDL, 1963

Once again I marveled at the sense of curiosity gorillas possess.

DIAN FOSSEY

FEW ANIMALS HAVE CAPTURED the public imagination more than gorillas, the largest of the great apes and the largest living primates. Like elephants, whales, lions, tigers, and polar bears, gorillas are charismatic megafauna, among nature's largest living creatures in the animal kingdom. The public can't seem to get enough of them. In fact, gorillas were the first apes known to the Western world. The first mention of any great ape in the written records of Western civilization occurred in 470 BC, when a group of colonists reached West Africa. There the colonists killed three females the locals called "gorillas." The dead gorillas were flayed and their skins brought back to Carthage where they were displayed at the Melkarth Temple dedicated to Juno.

Two thousand years passed before Western civilization encountered gorillas again. This time their size and alleged ferocity left a more permanent impression. Reports of large, hairy creatures, perhaps part human but exceptionally strong and aggressive, fit prevailing images of Africa, the so-called dark continent.

Not until the mid-nineteenth century did the stories of the hairy "gorilli" begin to be accepted as more fact than fiction. In 1847 a Christian missionary, Thomas Savage, collaborated with an anatomist, publishing a detailed description based on a single skull from Gabon and reports gathered in Africa. Even then there was confusion distinguishing between the great apes. Although the gorilla was finally declared separate from the other great apes, it was still termed a "new species of orang."

Unfortunately, Savage emphasized the gorilla's size and savagery, describing the male's "indescribable ferocity" and emphasizing that while hunting gorillas, if the gun failed to go off, the encounter could easily be fatal for the hunter. But the American big game hunter and traveler, Paul du Chaillu, probably did more than any other person to perpetuate the myth of the brutish, blood-thirsty gorilla. Chaillu was also frank in suggesting that part of the thrill of killing gorillas resided in the "dreadful note of human agony" that accompanied their deaths. The vicarious thrill of killing something almost human resonates in his books, in which he recounted his exploits killing these "hellish dream creatures . . . half man, half beast." These books attracted much attention and laid the foundation for the general belief that gorillas are monsters of nature. Museum displays and statues of large male gorillas mounted on their hind legs as if ready to charge, with their teeth bared and mouths foaming, also contributed to the image of a mighty "man-eating beast."

This image culminated in the film *King Kong,* which became the highest grossing film of 1933. The story of King Kong is essentially a more vigorous, brutalized version of the old European folktale "Beauty and the Beast." King Kong was 50 feet tall, king of the gorillas, to whom African villagers sacrificed beautiful maidens. He was captured and brought to North America where he escaped, climbed the Empire State Building, and was brought down by machine gun fire shot from airplanes. His downfall was caused by his love for the glamorous blonde Fay Wray.

The myth of the brutal ape was perpetuated in films like *King Kong,* but it still lives on today. Best-selling author Michael Crichton's book *Congo,* with its good gorillas (including the signing gorilla heroine) and its evil gorillas—a Hollywood blockbuster movie in the 1990s—may have reinterpreted the stereotypes, but it failed to eliminate them. As recently as 2003, while I was at a zoo taking a picture of an adult male gorilla, a Korean tourist who spoke only a bit of English came up to me, smiled, pointed at the large ape and said, "King Kong!"

The gorilla is not only the largest living primate, it is also the largest of all primates known to science. (The fossil *Gigantopithecus* has equally large teeth but its actual body dimensions and weight are not known.) How large are gorillas? Very large, indeed. Some male gorillas have weighed over 500 pounds and stood over six feet tall when upright. Gorillas now

occupy a truncated geographical range along the equatorial belt of Africa. Although gorillas are sometimes placed in the same genus as the chimpanzee *Pan,* more conventionally they are classified as the genus *Gorilla* with one species *gorilla*. Traditionally taxonomists classified gorillas as consisting of three subspecies: the western lowland (*G. g. gorilla*), the eastern lowland (*G. g. graueri*), and the mountain gorilla (*G. g. beringei*). The western lowland gorillas are physically the smallest but have the widest distribution, being found in Congo Brazzaville, Gabon, Equatorial Guinea, Cameroon, and Central African Republic. The eastern lowland gorilla is only encountered in eastern Democratic Republic of Congo (the former Zaire). Mountain gorillas are found in the Virunga Volcanoes, a mountainous triangle shared by the Democratic Republic of Congo, Uganda, and Rwanda. They are found in only one other place, the Bwindi Impenetrable Park of Uganda, which is 22 miles to the south of the Volcanoes at altitudes of 4,000 to 7,000 feet. Although the Bwindi gorillas' status as mountain gorillas has been questioned, genetic data indicate that the Bwindi population is indistinguishable from the gorillas in the Virunga Volcanoes.

Time and isolation have brought on minor differences among the three subspecies. The two lowland species are separated by over 625 miles, but the consensus is that they may once have been contiguous. The eastern lowland and mountain gorillas have developed very black hair compared to the gray and even reddish coats of the western lowland gorillas, and their teeth and jaws are larger. The eastern lowland gorillas, also called Grauer's gorilla, are the largest gorillas with adult males averaging 360 pounds in weight and males as large as 500 pounds reported from captivity. The mountain gorilla—distinguished from the other two species by its longer body hair, broader chest, and shorter arms as well as a slightly more humanlike foot—is the rarest subspecies.

Mountain gorillas were not scientifically documented until 1902 when a German captain, Oscar von Beringe, shot two mountain gorillas and sent back a skeleton of one to be examined in Europe. The scientific name it came back with was his own, *G. g. beringei*. In recent years some taxonomists have recognized two gorilla species, *G. g. beringei* and *G. g. gorilla*, with four or five subspecies. Three of the five newly proposed subspecies are classified as critically endangered while the other two, including western lowland gorillas, are endangered. Wild gorillas are increasingly found in fragmented and isolated small populations. Under the newly proposed classification of five subspecies, the Cross River gorilla, found only in Nigeria and Cameroon, has less than 200 individuals remaining, while the mountain gorillas in the Virungas may number only about 300 and the Bwindi gorillas under 300. Western lowland gorillas may number 100,000 individuals, by far the largest number for any gorilla subspecies in the wild. Nonetheless, this represents

a far smaller number than in the past and suggests that the future will not be bright for any gorilla subspecies. Due to *National Geographic* articles and films about Dian Fossey's work with gorillas and the eco-tourism developed in the Virunga Volcanoes region, mountain gorillas are the best-known gorillas. But virtually all gorillas in captivity and most whose remains are on display or stored in museums are western lowland gorillas.

Early field reports about gorillas were written by great white hunters like Chaillu. Not surprisingly, these men provoked the rage they described so vividly. In the late 1950s George Schaller, a lean and stern-looking American zoologist, conducted the first scientific study of gorillas. Writer and naturalist Peter Matthiessen portrayed Schaller as a man not much seen but whose presence is deeply felt, much like the shadowy subject of Matthiessen's book, *The Snow Leopard*. In his groundbreaking study, Schaller overcame the gorillas' fear and resistance by wearing drab clothing and by resolutely and quietly tracking them until they finally learned to accept him. Jane Goodall once told me that when she first met Schaller, shortly after she began her own pioneering work, she followed him around awestruck because he had gotten close enough to actually observe wild mountain gorillas while at that point she couldn't get within half a mile of the chimpanzees she was trying to study.

But not until the long-term studies of Dian Fossey did attitudes toward gorillas begin to change. Almost singlehandedly, Fossey dissolved the man-eater image and replaced it with that of the gentle giant. Fossey published articles in *National Geographic*, wrote the popular book *Gorillas in the Mist,* and attracted major media attention as she lectured extensively throughout North America. After Fossey's brutal murder, the film, based on the book with Sigourney Weaver in the title role, was instrumental in sealing the public's approval of gorillas. With extensive documentation, Fossey revealed gorillas as gentle vegetarians and the allegedly fearsome and ferocious adult males as gentle and caring fathers.

Unlike chimpanzees and orangutans, gorillas spend much of their time on the ground. Perhaps this is due to their large size and their ecology. For instance, mountain gorillas who are particularly terrestrial spend 97 percent of their time on the ground. Like the other African apes, robust and gracile chimpanzees, gorillas knuckle-walk. Knuckle-walking is a unique form of quadrupedal ground locomotion in which much of the body's weight is placed on the knuckles of the hand. Gorillas rarely stand upright or walk bipedally. However, bipedal standing and charging are important components of the adult male gorilla's chest-beating displays that so impressed the Victorian explorers and naturalists, displays which helped give gorillas their initial reputation as mighty and ferocious beasts. Among gorillas there seems to be an inverse correlation between arboreal behavior and body size. Gorillas rarely brachiate (swinging,

An adolescent mountain gorilla checks out the photographer in the Virunga Volcanoes. Mountain gorillas are distinguished from other populations of gorillas by their long black hair, as seen on this young male.

suspended, hand over hand) or jump in the trees; rather, they are basically quadrupedal climbers. Gorillas also sleep on the forest floor, nearly always making their night nests on the ground. Adult gorillas are very cautious in trees, but juveniles seem at home in the canopy, playing, exploring, resting, and feeding there with apparent ease.

Their terrestiality does not make gorillas easier to study. In the case of the mountain gorillas, the favored habitat tends to be extremely dense. An observer can be three feet from a wild gorilla, can even hear and smell the individual but still may not be able to see him or her. A surprised or frightened gorilla can be a dangerous one. Fossey habituated gorillas with introductory and feeding vocalizations. These were vocalizations the gorillas themselves use to express fullness and contentment. Thus, as they came to know her voice, she was able to get quite near them without surprising them. Fossey became expert at gorilla vocalizations. Her demonstrations of this unique skill at public lectures never failed to delight audiences. After the pioneering work of Schaller and the in-depth study by Fossey, a number of researchers contributed to our understanding of gorilla ecology and social organization, among them Kelly Stewart, Alexander (Sandy) Harcourt, Sabater Pi, David Watts, Michele Goldsmith, Caroline Tutin, Juichi Yamagiwa, Peter Veit, and Takakazu Yumoto.

Throughout their range, wild gorillas show similar patterns of social organization. They usually live in relatively stable family groups of adult males and females, with solitary males comprising about ten percent of the population. Lone females are virtually never seen. The family group may number from two to fifty-one members, as has been recently observed in the Virungas, but the average size is between five and twelve members. In West Africa the size of the group tends to be smaller than among the eastern gorilla subspecies. But the number is not due to fewer males but rather to fewer females and immature individuals in the group. Approximately 60 percent of gorilla groups have only one adult male. In fact, groups with more adult males do not necessarily have more females.

Adult male gorillas are distinguished from others in the group not only by their large size, adult males being twice the size of females, but also by the silver or gray saddle of hair that runs down male backs and flanks. Thus, adult male gorillas are known as silverbacks. The younger males of about eight to fourteen years of age may attain large size but not the white saddles of hair, and so are called blackbacks. The maximum number of silverbacks ever seen in a bisexual group until recently is four (although Fossey observed a group of five males, both silverbacks and blackbacks, who traveled together after the lone female in the group died of old age). However, in the past few years a group with eight silverbacks was observed in the Virunga Volcanoes.

A silverback mountain gorilla screams as he mock charges an intruder. Gorillas rarely charge with the intent to harm, unless the individual being charged turns and runs. That is why some African peoples traditionally regarded a person who had been bitten by a gorilla as a coward.

LEFT
Happy at last: Two rescued gorilla youngsters at play. Due to their small size and agility, young gorillas are more likely than adults to go up into the trees to forage for food, to nest, and to play.

ABOVE
The trauma that orphaned youngsters like this one suffer when their mothers and families are killed for the bushmeat trade is obvious. The development of an infrastructure by logging companies and the prevalence of guns in the war-torn Congo Basin has led to the commercialization of the bushmeat trade to such an extent that vast quantities of bushmeat are efficiently harvested by professional hunters and sent out to large urban centers.

OPPOSITE
The western lowland gorillas are smaller than the mountain gorillas and their hair has a reddish hue. Here a western lowland silverback reposes in all his majesty.

A mountain gorilla's hands
are much like ours, and
among great apes, the
mountain gorilla's foot is
most similar to a human's,
with the big toe less diver-
gent than the big toes of
other apes. Perhaps this is
because mountain gorillas
spend more of their time
on the ground. Silverbacks
rarely climb into the canopy
except to forage when prized
food species are available.

A silverback vocalizes in the
Virunga Volcanoes. Adult
males are twice the size of
females, making gorillas
one of the most sexually
dimorphic of primates. Adult
males also have internal air
sacs over their ribs. This
allows the males to give
their chest-beating displays
without fracturing their
ribs. These air sacs may also
serve as resonating cham-
bers for the chest-beating.

Two mountain gorillas from
different groups interact
aggressively. During such
encounters, Fossey discovered, female gorillas sometimes change groups. In a
few cases, adult female
gorillas even transferred to
other groups, leaving their
youngsters behind in the
original group with their
silverback father.

The gorilla is one of the few primates in which both males
and females typically leave their natal groups after puberty.
Among the mountain gorillas, adolescent or young adult
females transfer directly to another group or attach themselves
to a solitary silverback. Females initiate transfer when two
groups encounter one another or a group meets a solitary
male. While the silverbacks in the two groups fight or charge
each other, the female may leave her group, approach a silverback from the other group (or a solitary) and then follow him
after the encounter ends. Most females change groups as often
as eight times before they find a silverback that satisfies them
in some way. Usually females change groups in their youth,
frequently before their first pregnancy, but occasionally they
will leave their juvenile offspring behind with the presumed
father and his group.

Being selective about partners is not limited to gorillas in
the wild. Even in captivity male and female gorillas brought
together in the hopes that they will mate sometimes don't. A
good example is Demba and Chaka at the Philadelphia Zoo.
Introduced to each other with high hopes among zoo management for the gorillas' reproductive success, after five years
female Demba had not mated with Chaka. Chaka fathered eight
offspring at the Cincinnati Zoo and is one of the world's most
prolific gorillas, yet seemed unable to convince Demba to mate.
Zoo management claims that the hand-reared Demba simply
isn't comfortable with gorillas. However, it could be just a
matter of female choice. Perhaps another male would interest
Demba enough to mate.

Despite the presence of four and occasionally more adult
males in a group, there always seems to be one dominant
silverback that is the undisputed leader of the group and presumably the father of most immatures in the group. Like the
females, male gorillas usually leave their natal group while still
blackbacks, before they have begun their reproductive years.
But, unlike females, they rarely join other mixed-sex or breeding
groups. Although blackbacks have been seen to transfer into
breeding groups, this is rare. Rather when males leave their natal
group, they tend to be solitary until they start their own groups
by attracting one or more females, or form all-male groups.
Among observed mountain gorillas, more than ten percent of all
groups of two or more animals consist exclusively of males. In
the Virunga Volcanoes, four occasionally observed males were
each still alone two to five years after they left their birth group.
They sometimes briefly associated with females and sometimes
with another lone male. The most consistently observed lone
male was still alone three years after he left his group.

Since males so rarely transfer to another silverback's group,
in the 40 percent or so of cases where there is more than one
silverback in a group, the males are probably all closely related.
Perhaps it is easier to wait for daddy silverback to become
senile and die, especially if he's already faltering, than to go

out into the world, start from scratch, and begin competing to attract females. Although males typically leave their groups upon becoming blackbacks, some males never leave the groups into which they are born.

Why do males leave at all? The answer probably lies in the fact that the life of adult male gorillas is characterized by fierce male-male competition for access to females. A stable gorilla family group usually consists of a silverback male and several adult females and their offspring. One silverback and one female is not a stable unit. If the silverback cannot attract more females, the female will leave him. We don't know precisely why this is so. But the male has no choice but to compete with other males. Since females always stay in groups led by a silverback, silverbacks recruit females from the female's natal family group or from other males during intergroup encounters.

Among mountain gorillas, over three quarters of observed encounters between males entailed intense threat displays, particularly chest-beatings, while half of observed encounters involved fights or combats with physical contact. Such intense male-male competition for females probably helps explain the extreme sexual dimorphism found in gorillas. Males not only weigh twice as much as females (200-pound females versus 350–400-pound males in the wild), they also have a more massive musculature and much larger canines.

These activities, intense male-male competition, males and females leaving their birth groups, and females recruited during intergroup encounters seem typical of gorillas wherever they have been observed in the wild. The protectiveness of the silverback towards his females and their offspring is also evident in captivity. I remember a silverback male at the Denver Zoo standing behind the glass at the front of the gorilla enclosure, alert, every muscle taut, watching the humans with a wary, almost angry eye, while the females lounged in the background. Clearly, the females were aware that the male was on guard watching out for them. Here was a gorilla who took his family responsibilities very seriously. No wonder silverbacks in captivity have relatively high mortality rates and don't even reproduce very well: it is probably the stress of being "on" all the time.

I had another experience with an adult male gorilla in a zoo in Kansas. I was allowed to go behind the cages to feed raisins to an adult male orangutan whom I had just met. In the benign, unemotional manner of orangutans, the male opened his lips and let me pop raisins directly into his mouth. He was relaxed and cordial; he had absolutely nothing to prove to me or anyone else. He just wanted the raisins. I didn't fool myself into thinking that the interaction was about me and him; it wasn't. It was about just him and the raisins. Across the way, I heard loud banging. An adult male gorilla was throwing himself against the bars of his cage. The keeper said "I think he wants some raisins, too." So I went over and placed some raisins onto

a horizontal bar of his cage and then moved away. (I didn't dare put them directly into his mouth). The gorilla put on a magnificent display for several minutes before he finally condescended to come close and take the raisins. Before he accepted my raisins, he had to impress me with his male gorillahood. Even though I was giving him a treat, it must have been stressful for him. He charged so violently that I thought the bars might pop out of the cage.

The late Dian Fossey wrote about the "highly protective strategies of a group's silverback leader." Once, while she was climbing through tall foliage up a steep mountainside, she suddenly came upon Group 8, one of her habituated gorilla groups, a group which accepted her. Group 8 was an unusual group: first because it initially consisted of five males, a very distinguished-looking heavily silvered old male, a young silverback, three younger blackbacks, and a doddering old female. The dignified older silverback, Rafiki, and the female, Coco, often shared the same night nest. Second, since this group had no young to protect, they accepted Fossey's presence almost instantaneously with great serenity. In fact, Peanuts, one of the younger male gorillas in the group, was the first wild gorilla ever to touch Dian. Jubilant, when Dian returned to camp, she sent Louis Leakey a telegram saying "I've finally been accepted by a gorilla." It was this very same cable that Louis Leakey carried in his shirt pocket the day I first met him at UCLA; he alluded to it during a question and answer period when he spoke about having encouraged both Jane Goodall and Dian Fossey to study chimpanzees and gorillas. Fossey was thrilled when I told her about Louis patting the pocket holding the telegram the first time I heard him speak.

One day Fossey inadvertently surprised Group 8 by abruptly coming upon them from below the mountain: "Suddenly, like a pane of broken glass, the air around me was shattered by the screams of the five males of the group as they bulldozed their way down through the foliage towards me. . . . The intensity of the gorillas' screams was so deafening, I could not locate the source of the noise. I only knew that the group was charging from above, when the tall vegetation gave way as though an out-of-control tractor were headed directly for me."

Since the vegetation was so thick, the silverback only recognized Dian when he was within three feet of her and quickly braked to a stop, causing the four charging males behind him to pile into his back. Dian saved herself by sinking to the ground and assuming the most submissive pose that she could muster. The five males stood over her for half an hour, screaming if she so much as moved a muscle, before finally moving back uphill.

Dian related other incidents, including one in which a person who had worked with gorillas for a year approached two interacting groups from below. One of the silverbacks, probably already in a bad mood from the interaction with the other

An eastern lowland silverback heads out for a stroll, the white saddle on his back barely visible from this angle.

TOP
A familiar sight among gorillas: A wild eastern lowland male sitting patiently with a youngster. The silverback's high domed head consists of a bony saggital crest on top of the skull that anchors powerful chewing muscles.

BOTTOM
A wild female gorilla watches intently as her youngster climbs into the canopy while she herself remains on the ground. Although half the size of a silverback, female gorillas are primarily terrestrial, even making their night nests on the ground.

group, saw the researcher and immediately charged him, rolled with him for 30 feet down the hill, breaking three of the man's ribs. The gorilla then bit into the back of the man's neck. Had the bite been on the front of his neck rather than behind, he almost certainly would have died. But Dian emphasized that these "charge anecdotes" do gorillas a disservice. Normally, silverbacks only charge when defending their families against other gorilla males. Charging at people is the result of human encroachment into gorilla habitat. Had human encroachment been rarer, gorillas would probably have hidden rather than charged. Dian had no sympathy for people who didn't follow gorilla etiquette.

Dian taught her students to vocalize when approaching wild gorillas. This reduced the possibility of surprise and subsequent outbursts. On warm sunny days, as gorillas peacefully rest and feed among their family groups, they emit soft purring sounds that resemble stomachs rumbling. Dian named these "belch vocalizations." These sounds epitomized gorilla well-being to Dian, especially since one animal expressing a series of belch vocalizations almost invariably induced a chain of responses from other nearby gorillas. This sound was the perfect way for Dian to alert gorilla groups to her presence, while demonstrating her own peaceful intentions and feelings of well-being.

Unlike all other great apes, gorillas have been characterized as folivorous, or foliage-eating. This characterization is based on the long-term studies initiated by Dian Fossey and her colleagues on mountain gorillas living on the Virunga Volcanoes. But mountain gorillas may not represent all gorillas in terms of their ecology, particularly the smaller western lowland gorillas who live in tropical rain forests at low altitudes and whose groups are smaller. Mountain gorillas live on the edge of their historic range. As people and horticulture have ascended the slopes of Mt. Visoke and the other mountains of the Virunga range, the mountain gorillas have been forced even higher. What these gorillas are observed doing may not exactly reflect the strategies they used in the past.

The herbaceous diet of gorillas has advantages and disadvantages. Vegetation is relatively low in calories, uses more energy to digest, and sometimes contains toxins. On the other hand, herbaceous vegetation and young leaves are high in protein, abundant and evenly distributed throughout the habitat, and available year-round. As a result, gorillas do not need to travel far each day to find food. It has even been suggested that the large body mass of gorillas (for females two or three times the size of other ape females) represents a new digestive strategy in that their large body sizes allow gorillas to prosper on vast quantities of relatively low-calorie foods. Such animals can also live together in large groups without severely competing with each other for food.

This contrasts with the situation facing fruit-eaters like the chimpanzees. Ripe fruit is easily digested, high in water and sugars, high in energy, and low in toxins. But ripe fruit is also low in protein, unevenly distributed in patches throughout the habitat, and almost always available only seasonally. Fruit-eaters usually must travel great distances to forage for food. As a result, members of large groups may exhibit a "fission-fusion" type of social organization, in which temporary feeding groups vary in size but remain part of a community. But this community virtually never comes together as a unit because there is not enough food in one place to feed everybody.

In the Virunga Volcanoes, gorillas do not compete with chimpanzees, which are totally absent there, probably due to the lack of fruit. In other areas, even in Bwindi, where gorillas live at lower elevations and chimpanzees are present, there is a great deal of more seasonally available fruit. Gorillas in these habitats eat more fruit, travel longer distances per day, and spend more time feeding and resting in trees. Western lowland gorillas eat more fruit and travel farther per day than Bwindi gorillas.

Michele Goldsmith, who studied gorillas in the Central African Republic, suggests that altitude has great bearing on gorilla ecology and even social behavior. At low altitudes, forests are rich in fruit and chimpanzee densities are high. Here gorillas are more frugivorous (eat more fruit), more arboreal, travel longer distances daily, and may even have somewhat less cohesive groups as they must spread out to feed on widely dispersed fruit trees. But at high altitudes as in the Virunga Volcanoes where fruit resources are few and far between (and thus no chimpanzees), gorillas are folivorous, terrestrial, and travel very short daily distances, according to David Watts. These gorillas form the stable tight-knit groups so well described by Fossey, Stewart, and others. But even in the lowlands, gorillas consume large amounts of herbaceous and woody vegetation such as bark, young leaves, stems, and pith in addition to fruit. Sometimes over 90 percent of fecal samples from lowland gorillas contain leaves and fiber. However, in the Virungas, when fruit briefly becomes available, Dian Fossey was surprised to see august silverbacks climbing into the trees to feed on the ripe morsels.

Competition with robust chimpanzees may play an important role in gorilla adaptation. Throughout equatorial Africa, gorillas and chimpanzees are widely found in the same areas (except in the Virunga Volcanoes) with extensive overlaps in ranges and diet. Gorillas and chimpanzees occasionally cross paths in the same fruit trees. However, both species avoid contact with each other and do not respond aggressively to each other's presence. Robust chimpanzees and gorillas react very differently to fruit scarcity. When fruit is abundant, both species concentrate on fruit; when fruit is scarce, gorillas increase the herbaceous and woody content of their diet, concentrating almost exclusively on ground plants, pith, leaves, and bark, and their range size decreases. Interestingly, as gorillas travel less during times of fruit scarcity, the rate of encounters with other gorillas probably decreases, meaning that females have less chance of changing groups. Chimpanzees, in contrast, disperse and continue seeking out fruit, expanding their day and month ranges and decreasing the size of their foraging parties. In many cases, figs constitute the "fall-back" fruit for chimpanzees.

Gorillas do not use or make tools in the wild (aside from nests) but have done so occasionally in captivity. Chimpanzees, on the other hand, are tool users and tool makers par excellence in the nonhuman animal kingdom. In the wild, tool making and tool use enable chimpanzees to feed on high quality, energy-rich foods, such as nuts and oil-palm piths, which are protected by hard shells or very fibrous tissue, as well as insects embedded in large nests or insects too dangerous to handle directly. Even during seasons of fruit scarcity, tool use expands the diversity of the chimpanzee diet.

During the course of evolution, interspecies competition between gorillas and robust chimpanzees probably accelerated niche separation and promoted different foraging strategies, especially during times of seasonal food scarcity (no fruit, no flowers). When the availability of fruit decreases, gorillas minimize their expenditure of energy by switching to vegetative foods. Chimpanzees try to stick to fruit and correspondingly increase their expenditure of energy by traveling longer distances in order to find it. Flexibility in terms of diet and lack of territoriality (territoriality being very characteristic of robust chimpanzees) allows gorillas greater flexibility over various habitats and seasons. Perhaps it could be argued that gorillas are thus more successful, evolutionarily speaking, than chimpanzees. Gorillas show some specializations in their jaws and associated muscles, which are probably related to the extreme foliovory of the mountain gorillas.

What about the gracile chimpanzees, bonobos? Through some accident of geography, ancestral bonobos were liberated from competition with gorillas. There are no gorillas south of the Congo River where gracile chimpanzees are found. A decade ago Richard Wrangham suggested that the loss of gorillas 1.5–2.5 million years ago within the range of some ancestral chimpanzee-like populations made abundant protein-rich foliage more available to the ancestral bonobos than to ancestral robust chimpanzees. Thus, bonobos do not have to compete with gorillas. Bonobos eat more foliage than robust chimpanzees. Bonobos have access to the resources available to both chimpanzees and gorillas in other areas. They are doubly rich. This relative lack of food competition allows for larger and more stable bonobo groups, which, in turn, makes many kinds of aggression more dangerous and less beneficial to the aggressors. Wrangham concludes that, in the end, it reduced the propensity for "demonic male" aggression among bonobos, an aggression allegedly characteristic of both robust chimpanzees and gorillas as well as humans. This change in the costs of violence led ultimately to a proliferation of female-female alliances, an explosion of sexuality, and an absence of male-male coalitions as well as reduced individual vulnerability to attacks by gangs of males. This marked reduction in the propensity for male violence led to a great ape society, some have argued, unlike any other. The absence of gorillas south of the Congo River produced what Takayoshi Kano, a pioneer in the study of gracile chimpanzees, termed the bonobo's "peaceable kingdom." But contrary to stereotypes, male-male combat is relatively infrequent among gorillas that have access to ample ranges. Thus, in their own world, gorillas, too, created peaceable kingdoms, kingdoms that, unfortunately, may not survive the onslaught of human forces unleashed by the modern world.

ORANGUTANS: THE GREAT ORANGE APE

The Monkeys, Apes, and Baboons are of many different Sorts and Shapes; but the most remarkable are those they call Oran-ootans, which in their language signifies Men of the Woods.

DANIEL BEECKMAN, 1714, CITED IN
BARBARA HARRISSON (1962)

. . . one of the world's most delightful and rare animals . . .
L. WILLIAMS

ORANGUTANS HAVE ALWAYS BEEN the odd ape out. Unlike the African chimpanzees and gorillas, orangutans live only in Asia where their distribution is restricted to two large tropical islands, Sumatra and Borneo. In Sumatra orangutans range through some areas of the two Indonesian provinces of Aceh and Sumatra Utara (North Sumatra), which are located in the northernmost area of the island. On Borneo orangutans live in parts of the three Indonesian provinces of East, West, and Central Kalimantan as well as in the Malaysian states of Sabah and Sarawak. The largest orangutan populations are found in Kalimantan Tengah (Central Indonesian Borneo). During the Pleistocene, however, orangutans ranged as far north as southern China, throughout continental Southeast Asia, to the island of Java, and into southern Sumatra. Tooth size indicates that these Pleistocene orangutans may have been larger than present day orangutans.

If chimpanzees and gorillas are our sibling species, orangutans are first cousins, sharing more than 97 percent of our

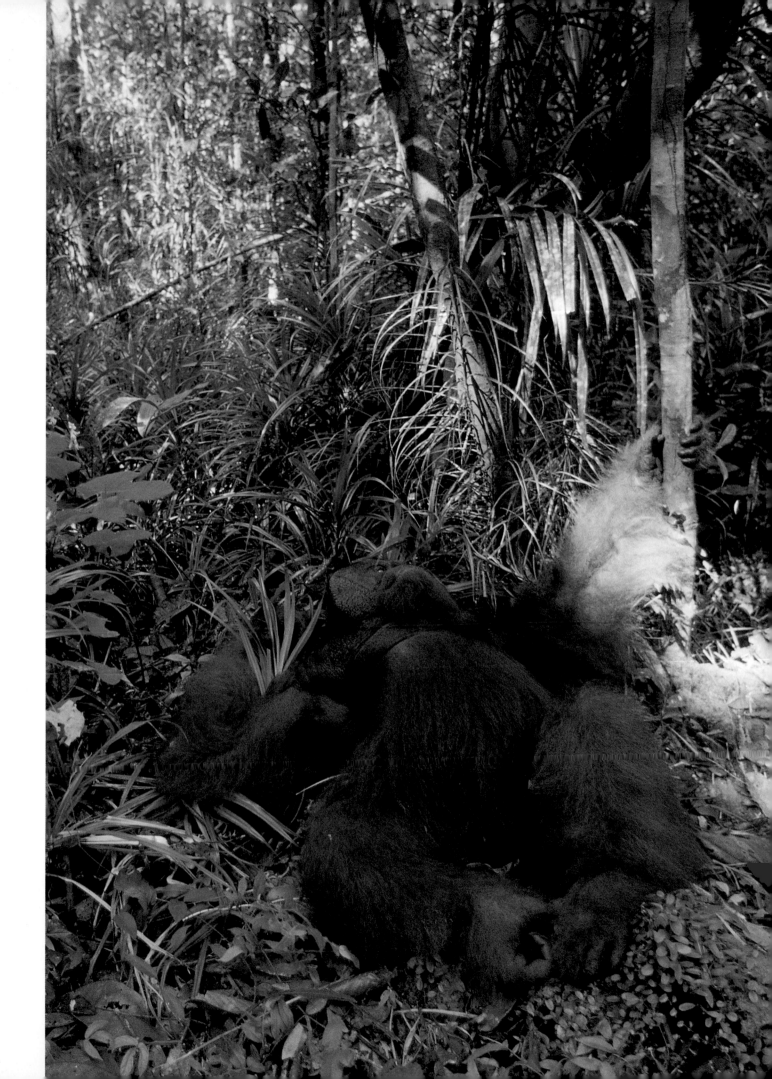

OPPOSITE
Camp Leakey's landmark
50-foot-high tower serves
as a platform from which
this photo was taken of the
Sekonyer Kanan River. The
Sekonyer Kanan is a typical
blackwater river running
through peat swamp forest.
The characteristic tea color
of the water comes from
organic acids in vegetation
dissolved in the water.

RIGHT
Although primarily arbo-
real, Bornean adult males
are also very much at ease
on the ground. The lack of
large territorial predators
such as tigers, which are
found in Sumatra but not in
Borneo, probably accounts
for Bornean orangutans
being more ground-living
than Sumatran orangutans.
Here Kusasi has flopped
down on the forest floor
for a short midday nap
without bothering to make
a day nest.

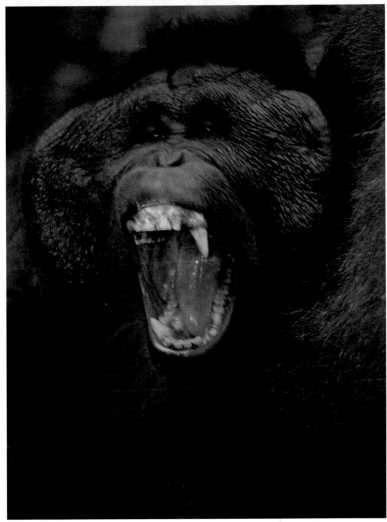

LEFT
Kusasi, locally known as
the King, is a cheekpadded
adult male orangutan. He
has been the dominant male
for over a decade in the
tropical rain forests adjacent
to Camp Leakey.

ABOVE
Two decades of fighting
other males has established
Kusasi as the dominant
male, and led to the loss of
two of his canines. But unlike
some other adult males,
Kusasi still has his fingers
and toes intact. When Kusasi
yawns, it is occasionally a
sign of frustration and unease
when he's not quite sure
what to do. The yawn also
shows off to any potential
foes in the vicinity the for-
midable fighting apparatus
he still carries in his jaws.

genetic material. For most of evolutionary history, humans, gorillas, and chimpanzees evolved side-by-side, adapting to changing environments in Africa. Although the earliest ancestral orangutan fossils are found in Africa, about 14 million years ago some ancestral orangutans left Africa for Asia. Whereas our own ancestors adapted to life on the ground, and gorillas and chimpanzees to a semi-terrestrial lifestyle, orangutans remained primarily arboreal, or tree dwelling.

In contrast to the black coats of African apes, orangutans have shaggy red hair, ranging from strawberry blonde, mostly in Sumatra, to a deep auburn in Borneo, and do not display secondary adaptations to terrestrial locomotion. In other words, since they spend so much time in the trees, they do not knuckle-walk, as do their African ape cousins. Gorillas are essentially ground-moving apes while chimpanzees, both gracile and robust, spend at least half of their daily activities on the ground.

In full sunlight, orangutans positively glow, but their skin is actually quite dark, so when they retreat into the shadows of the forest, they virtually disappear. Only the sound of cracking branches and falling fruit or shadowy movement in the treetops betrays their presence. This now-you-see-me, now-you-don't disappearing act is enhanced by the fact that orangutans are largely silent, unlike the garrulous chimpanzees and occasionally vocal gorillas. Orangutans are semi-solitary or, in the case of adult males, almost completely solitary. The gregarious chimpanzees frequently gather in large, noisy groups, especially when they discover a tree full of fruit. Gorillas live in tight-knit extended families, frequently dominated by a single mature silverback male. By comparison, orangutans are loners.

Orangutans are also among the most sexually dimorphic of all primates. Adult males are typically twice the size of females and may attain a height of four and a half feet or even five feet when standing erect. There is a record of an adult male who was shot and when measured, turned out to be over six feet tall. At full sexual maturity males develop wide cheekpads, a unique feature among monkeys and apes, as well as loose throat pouches. Males and females differ so much in size that local people viewed them as different creatures. Dayaks, the native people of Borneo, have several different words for orangutans, differentiating between cheekpadded males and non-cheekpadded females and subadult males. They further distinguish among cheekpadded males, naming them with different words depending on the size, shape, and stiffness of the cheekpads. Just as the Inuit reputedly use many different words for snow, and desert Arabs for camels, so some Dayak groups have at least five words for orangutans.

Conventionally scientists have divided Bornean and Sumatran orangutans into two subspecies: Bornean populations called *Pongo pygmaeus pygmaeus* and the Sumatran *Pongo pygmaeus abelii*. Some scientists have upgraded Sumatran and Bornean orangutan populations to full separate species status. One piece of evidence for an ancient bifurcation within orangutan populations is an inversion identified on chromosome two that appears to be correlated with the island of origin. Another is the absence of heterozygotes in natural populations. Also, recent analyses have documented other chromosome arrangements and revealed extraordinary degrees of variation in some genes, indicating that orangutan population structure is more complex than a simple dichotomy of Bornean and Sumatran populations. Some laboratory scientists have suggested that the two orangutan subspecies are as different from each other genetically as are gracile chimpanzees from robust, but this position is controversial. Currently, most orangutan specialists believe that there are four major populations or taxonomic groups of orangutans, three of them on Borneo and identified respectively as *Pongo pygmaeus pygmaeus, P. p. morio,* and *P. p. wurmbii,* as well as the Sumatran population. All four groupings should probably be treated equivalently so it may be possible that someday all four groupings will be elevated to species status.

Sumatran and Bornean orangutans are somewhat different in appearance. Bornean orangutans sometimes have brownish coats, which, in dim light, may look almost black. Sumatran orangutan hair is typically lighter, sometimes almost yellow. Sumatran orangutans, especially as infants or juveniles, often display a profusion of white hair on their faces. This is less common among Bornean orangutans. I have seen a few Sumatran infants whose yellow hair was virtually blonde: a lighter shade of pale. In addition, orangutans from Sumatra also seem to have thicker and softer hair than the Bornean.

At maturity, male Sumatran orangutans sometimes can be distinguished from the Bornean by their more pronounced beards, "Fu Manchu"–type moustaches, and generally hairier faces. Orangutan cheekpads may also differ between the two populations. In Borneo the cheekpads tend to grow more outward and forward, while in Sumatra the cheek flanges grow

As a subadult male, Kusasi crosses the Sekonyer Kanan River to get back to the Camp Leakey side. Orangutans have no fear of water. The author has observed wild orangutans up to their chins in water and others crossing rivers by using submerged logs as bridges. Years ago camp assistants rescued a juvenile ex-captive from drowning when he literally got in over his head trying to cross the Sekonyer Kanan. Although orangutans like water, they cannot swim.

sideways, giving the Sumatran males a flat-faced appearance that contrasts with the dish-faced Bornean male. However, since Bornean males are often more massive than Sumatran, this difference could also be a function of size, fatness, and musculature rather than genetics and inter-island variability.

But appearance does not warrant dividing orangutans into two separate species. We know that bonobos and robust chimpanzees are different not only because they look different, but also because their behaviors and ecologies are substantially different. Bornean and Sumatran orangutan behavior is similar. Ironically, before chromosomal analysis became available, people working with captive populations had trouble telling Sumatran and Bornean orangutans apart. Further, in captivity there are many fully viable Bornean-Sumatran crosses with second generation offspring fully fertile.

Like other great apes, orangutans do not have hair on their faces, or the palms of their hands and soles of their feet, or the top of their chests. Their dark tan or blackish skin is covered with relatively coarse and usually somewhat sparse hair. In addition to the different hues of Sumatran and Bornean populations, orangutan hair, like human hair, can be bleached by the sun. Years ago an adult female orangutan, a wildborn ex-captive named Rinnie, enjoyed sitting in the sun on the long causeway that links Camp Leakey to the Sekonyer Kanan River. Rinnie became the equivalent of a bleached blonde as her red hair took on bright brassy tones from the sun.

The skin or hair color of many infant primates changes as they grow older and gain maturity. Chimpanzee infants display a distinctive white tuft of hair on their behinds that disappears as they get older. Baboon infants are born with pink faces and ears and black coats that change to an adult coloration before they are a year old. Humans are no exception: My oldest son, Binti Paul, was platinum blond as a toddler. His fair skin and blond hair delighted local Indonesians who had never seen a blond baby before. Now, as a young adult, his hair is light brown or dark blond, depending on how much time he spends in the sun.

An orangutan infant's hair color is almost invariably lighter than his or her mother's hair. Sometimes the difference is startling. The greatest difference between orangutan adults and infants, however, are the prominent white patches around an infant's eye and mouth and scattered over his or her body. With some infants this is very subtle; with others, the effect resembles a piebald pony. As the infant ages, the patches become darker, and sometime during early adulthood, an orangutan's face and skin become quite dark, almost black. The darkness of facial patches is a rough but powerful gauge of an orangutan's age. Among wild orangutan females I have known, the face sometimes does not reach its full darkness until the female has given birth to her second infant, well into her twenties. Even then, a blink reveals white eyelids that may not disappear until

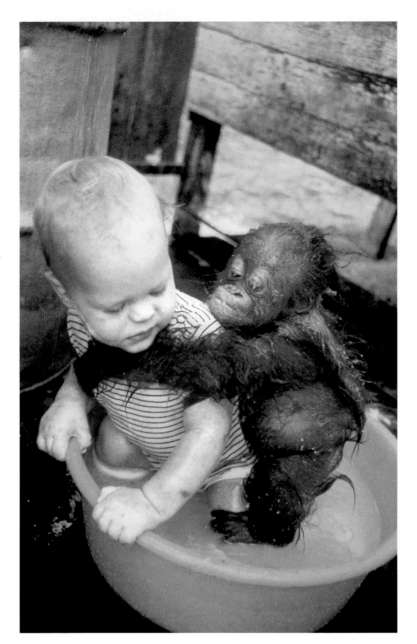

she is nearly thirty! Another sign of age is the hair. Some adult males and some older adult females may have partially or entirely bare backs. Throatpouch was the first wild adult male orangutan I habituated to my presence. Viewed from behind, he looked like someone had driven a lawn mower down the middle of his back!

Orangutans are not as powerfully built as gorillas, but they are larger than chimpanzees. In the wild adult males weigh as much as 200–300 pounds and females about 75–80 pounds. Captive orangutans often grow much faster and bigger than those in the wild. One two-and-a-half-year-old captive infant weighed over 40 pounds; in the wild, infants this age may be only five pounds! Older, obese adult males have reached 500 pounds in captivity. One such male was so fat that he couldn't walk and had a dome of subcutaneous fat on top of his head. There seems to be a greater tendency for orangutans, particularly Bornean ones, as opposed to chimpanzees and gorillas, to get fat in captivity. Fortunately, better management techniques and more careful husbandry of captive orangutans, particularly in North American zoos, have, in large part, corrected obesity problems.

Orangutan anatomy reflects the orangutan's arboreal existence. In contrast to African apes and humans, the orangutan's arms, hands, and feet are very long while their legs are short. Their trunks are round with a protruding belly that gives them a Humpty-Dumpty appearance. Another arboreal adaptation, unique to orangutans, is the flexible hip joints that allow orangutans similar movement in their legs and arms. Orangutans lack the ligament that binds the top of the leg to the hip; they can rotate their legs almost like a second set of arms. For an orangutan, doing splits and other acrobatic feats in the trees comes naturally, as does hanging upside down. Wild orangutans nonchalantly drink or eat while suspended by only one or two legs and juveniles will play-wrestle in this upside-down posture. Once I watched a 250-pound wild adult male briefly hang from a branch suspended by one and then two fingers, his legs dangling in the air, as he ate. Granted, these fingers were muscular and as plump as sausages. When I followed wild adult males, I would stare at those fingers and imagine their strength, especially if they were gripped around my throat, arm, or leg. I certainly would not have been able to escape their grasp! Having cared for ex-captive infants, I knew how strong even small orangutan babies can be. Although they weighed only a few pounds, when they clung to my body it was very difficult to remove them. My arms would become bruised black and blue from the clutching orangutan orphans. Local people claim that orangutan males are 40 times as strong as a human; in reality, I suspect that it is only eight times or so. And it isn't only the orangutan's grip that is so strong; gentle adult orangutans can crush and open a coconut with their jaws and teeth.

OPPOSITE

A wild orangutan female and her infant stare out from the forest near Camp Leakey, watching the activities carried out at the camp. Wild orangutans generally do not show much curiosity concerning humans or human activity. However, they are slightly more curious about the antics of ex-captive orangutans who are being rehabilitated at the camp.

RIGHT

The author's son, Binti Paul Brindamour, tries to take a bath with an infant orangutan, Princess, on his back. This image first appeared on the cover of *National Geographic Magazine* in June 1981 and has been reprinted numerous times since; it was even used as an album cover for a heavy metal band. Photograph by Rodney Brindamour.

When traveling through the forest canopy orangutans typically climb and clamber using a combination of hands and feet. Occasionally they swing through the trees hand-over-hand, suspended only by their long arms and hands. More typically, possibly because of their large size, they also grip a branch below with one or both feet. Orangutans frequently move through the trees by reaching out with one of their long arms, grasping a branch from another tree, pulling it toward themselves, and then using this branch to haul their large bodies into the next tree. Their hooklike hands have long palms and fingers with short thumbs low on the wrist. Their feet resemble their hands in having not only long soles and toes but also in having opposable big toes that are similar to the thumbs. When orangutans are sleeping in their tree nests with only one or two limbs protruding, it can be difficult to differentiate between hands and feet.

Orangutans seem to have an intuitive sense of physics. To cross gaps in the forest canopy and to move from one small tree to another, they use their weight to manipulate branches and pole trees (trees with small girths and most of their branches high up so that they resemble poles) and other vegetation. Holding on with an arm and one or two legs, they sway back and forth until the branch or pole tree swings like a pendulum in ever-greater arcs so that they reach the next tree. Sometimes orangutans climb as high as possible in a tree and then swing it back and forth until the entire tree sways far enough over for them to catch the next tree. When an adult male moves low in the canopy using pole tree trunks, he looks as if he is stilt walking! Standing erect, his weight is enough to bend pole trees so that he can catch the next one and move on. Despite adult males' substantial bulk, they are surprisingly supple and agile in the trees.

Females are also adept and agile in the trees even though much of the time they are carrying infants and even small juveniles. Females use their bodies to provide a bridge for their free-moving young. When a gap in the canopy is too large for a youngster moving behind his or her mother, she hangs horizontally between two trees, holding both simultaneously, so the youngster can safely cross by climbing over her body.

Although orangutans are primarily arboreal, mature wild Bornean males may spend up to six hours a day on the ground and even nest and sleep on the ground, but this is not typical behavior. Orangutans typically "walk" on closed fists or extended palms. Males can cover long distances moving rapidly on the ground, so quickly that sometimes it is difficult to keep up with them on uneven terrain. On level ground a human can sometimes keep up with them. At almost nine months pregnant, I outran a wild adult male who was behind me on the boardwalk leading to Camp Leakey. In the swamps, however, it was difficult to keep up with males even when I wasn't pregnant. Females come down to the ground less often and for

briefer periods. Nonetheless, both males and females have been encountered a considerable distance from the forest, especially when they are crossing open areas to get to the forest on the other side.

Bornean orangutans seem to spend more time on the ground than Sumatran orangutans. In Kalimantan I have almost bumped into wild orangutans on the ground. One possible explanation for this difference is the presence of large terrestrial predators such as tigers in Sumatra. While tigers are not found in Borneo, they are a very real presence in the forests and woodlands of Sumatra where they hunt primarily on the ground. In an area I surveyed with an Indonesian graduate student in mid-2003, a tiger had killed three villagers the month before and never been caught. The hair on the back of my neck stood on end when local villagers pointed out where they had seen a tiger in the previous few days. Another Indonesian student told me about suddenly coming face-to-face with a tiger as he hiked to an orangutan's nest in the early morning. The student was so shaken that he turned and ran straight back to camp, without even pausing to see the tiger's reaction! That Bornean adult male orangutans show so much ease and so little caution on the forest floor suggests that predators are not a major worry for them.

The words *orang hutan* in the Malay language mean "person of the forest" and are not necessarily restricted to orangutans but may refer to aboriginal hunter-gatherers. This ambiguity can be the source of confusion. In northern Sumatra, orangutans are called *mawas*. When I asked people in Sumatra about orangutans, some thought that I was referring to technologically primitive tribes (such as the Kubu and the Penan), not great red apes. The confusion goes both ways. My husband is a Dayak, one of the native people of Borneo who practice shifting cultivation and traditionally lived in the interior. When we were married twenty-five years ago, one of my Western friends in Jakarta was told, to his astonishment, that I had married an *orang hutan*: the speaker meant a native of Borneo, literally a person of the forest, but my friend thought he meant an ape. At that time, travel to Kalimantan from other islands in Indonesia was rare and communications, rudimentary. Many rural people from other parts of Indonesia thought that Dayaks had tails, probably because the men traditionally wore long narrow black loin cloths that flowed behind them gracefully as they moved. Not surprisingly, there was much confusion as to what *orang hutan* really were: tailed men, tailless red apes, or something else altogether! To add to the confusion, in the Malaysian state of Sabah on the northernmost tip of Borneo, local people sometimes refer to the native elephant as *orang hutan* or as the wise ones, out of deep respect for the creature.

Orangutans are diurnal. In Tanjung Puting National Park where I have studied them for 34 years, they spend on average 60 percent of their active waking time feeding, 18 percent rest-

ing, 20 percent traveling, and 2 percent in other activities, such as vocalizing, mating, and nest-building. Almost every evening wild orangutans construct a nest, a sleeping platform, in the trees by bending and breaking branches, leaves, and twigs. Occasionally orangutans make day nests to rest or, in the case of adult females, to hide from the attentions of an unwanted subadult male suitor. Occasionally orangutans reuse old nests, their own or someone else's, but usually add fresh green branches and foliage to the old structure. In Tanjung Puting they spend at least ten minutes constructing nests and frequently work twenty minutes or more on them. Unlike the African apes, orangutans use branches and leaves as overhead covers to protect themselves from the rain and the elements.

Orangutans are predominantly ripe fruit-eaters although they also feed on some unripe fruit, young leaves and shoots, flowers and buds, the inner bark of some lianas and trees, ground plants, vines, fungi, ants, termites, caterpillars, and one type of spider as well as small amounts of presumably mineral-rich soil. In Tanjung Puting National Park, over the last 34 years, we have cataloged 400 different foods. This variety is so high that one is tempted to describe orangutans as omnivorous and opportunistic foragers. But this would be misleading. In fact, orangutans are highly selective feeders. On average, 60 percent of their feeding time is devoted to fruit. Frequently, the ground below the trees where orangutans have fed is littered with rejected unripe or substandard fruit. Orangutans seem to prefer large crops of ripe fruit with soft sweet pulp, which provide their large bodies with easy calories and high energy content. In Sumatra orangutan densities are tightly correlated with the number of trees providing soft pulp fruit. Orangutans also like oily nuts that take large energy expenditures to open but may provide them with rare lipids. Orangutans will spend up to eight hours in a single tree opening up only a few nuts per hour with their teeth. Why not use a rock? Well, there is no rock in coastal Borneo. Even the crushed rock used in roads is imported!

On rare occasions, orangutans eat meat. At the Camp Leakey study site we saw an adult male swallow a handful of baby squirrels whole, without hesitation. Another time, an Indonesian student observed a subadult orangutan male eating an adult squirrel. This orangutan, too, ate the entire squirrel: not a shred of skin or bit of bone dropped to the ground. But these were isolated, apparently opportunistic, incidents. Bornean orangutans do not actively hunt for meat, as chimpanzees do.

Orangutans travel from less than 200 feet to three miles per day, usually ranging under one mile. In East Borneo the average day range is 1,000 feet while in Tanjung Puting orangutans range about half a mile per day. Males have more extensive home ranges than females. Around Camp Leakey, male home ranges exceed 30 square miles and are much larger than

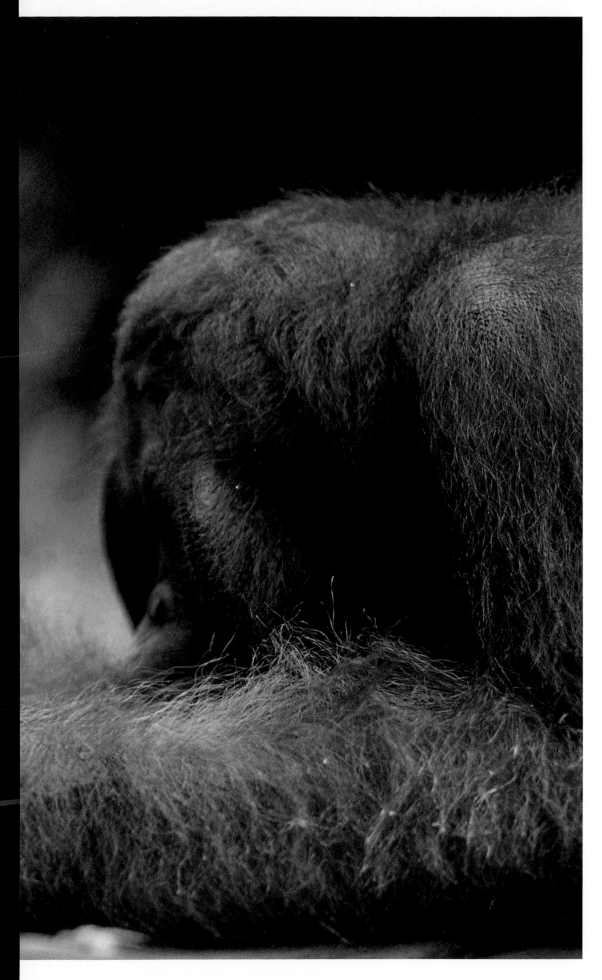

the size of the study area, while females have overlapping ranges of at least 8 square miles. In the entire 34 years of my study, not a single wild male stayed permanently within the study area. Most adult males stayed only a short time, while others set up their home ranges for the few years when they were dominant in the area. Thus males come and go while most females stay in the same areas from year to year.

There are two phases of sexual maturation among male orangutans, adult and subadult. In addition to their large size, adult males exhibit striking secondary sexual characteristics, particularly prominent cheekpads, which develop along the side of the face and enhance the size of the head. This has been linked with increased levels of testosterone. The cheekpads may have a megaphone function for the adult male's "long call," so-named by John McKinnon: a long-distance vocalization that can sometimes be heard over distances of one or two miles. But this function has not been proven, only suggested. Adult males also have throatpouches that serve as resonating chambers for this call. The long call usually lasts for a minute or more; calls up to five minutes in length have been documented. The long call typically begins with a throaty roar, a sound similar to a motorcycle starting up, then changes gradually, or sometimes abruptly, into a series of bellows, the loudest part of the call, which subsides into a series of gradually diminishing sighs. Local people say that the orangutan male is sighing because his bride left him on his wedding night, the reason why he is always alone. I have been within inches of wild adult males vocalizing long calls; the vibrations went through my body as though a train locomotive were going by. I don't know if this was produced by the sheer loudness of the call or if perhaps, like elephant sounds, there was a low-frequency component to the call that my human ears could not pick up but which my body could feel.

The long call acts as a general call to alert every other orangutan to his presence. Orangutans seemingly pay no heed to this call if the caller is more than several hundred yards away. However, other adult males may freeze or run away if the caller is close by, or, less often, move aggressively toward him. Females rarely react strongly to a male's long call. An adult female may slowly move in his direction or she may move away. The most intense reactions come from adolescent females who may move toward the adult male and visibly signal that they are interested in sex. In addition to the long call, adult male orangutans give a shorter, faster, more intense version I have termed the "fast call," which the caller specifically addresses to another adult male in the vicinity. The calling male is probably threatening the other male who is close to him. While vocalizing these calls, the calling male seems agitated and angry.

Females may vocalize a series of grunts and roars that at first seems as though they are about to break out into a full-

fledged long call, but they never duplicate the series of loud bellows vocalized by adult males. Females produce these loud calls when they are upset by the presence of another female or subadult male and occasionally when the female's juvenile offspring has wandered off. Orangutan females sometimes scream when they are being forcibly copulated with (in human terms, raped); these piercing screams may be very abrupt and are sometimes almost unbearable on the eardrums. Adult females also vocalize loud grunts, sometimes punctuated by shrieks or screams, in protest, while struggling against being raped. In a few cases, the screams or loud grunts resulted in other males appearing and, in the manner of gallant knights, rescuing the female from the rapist. Interestingly, during these occasions, the gallant male did not stay and did not mate with the female. Orangutans are one of the few animals where forcible copulations have been indubitably documented.

Subadult males lack the wide cheekpads, large size, and large throatpouches of the adult male and they generally do not long call. Although not as large or as husky as adult males, subadults are still as large as or larger than adult females. In the wild, subadults may remain in this state for 10 to 20 years. This arrested development has been linked with stress associated with the presence of adult males. Eventually, if they live long enough, all males seem to acquire the secondary sexual characteristics and size of adult males. If housed alone, like Rusty in the Albuquerque Zoo, males can become adult at the age of 13 in captivity or as late as 18 or 19 years of age. But in the wild males sometimes don't attain adulthood until they reach their twenties. Once they become fully adult, they will not tolerate the presence of another cheekpadded male. In the 20 or more "almost encounters" I have witnessed between two lone adult males, with few exceptions the males avoided meeting each other. In the few instances where they actually confronted one another, one of the males almost immediately fled. These very rare encounters among adult males contrast sharply with the hundreds of meetings I have witnessed among wild adult females, subadults, and adolescents.

Orangutan social organization is unique among monkeys and apes. Alone among higher primates, orangutans are semi-solitary. Adult males are the most solitary, associating only with their consorts, former consorts, and persistent potential consorts. The Bornean adult male makes some prosimians seem like paragons of social activity because he is alone so much of the time. If you exclude occasional brief encounters with females where the orangutans seem like two ships passing in the night, to quote David Agee Horr, then adult male orangutans spend over 95 percent of their time alone.

Adult females are more social than adult males as they are usually with one or two dependent young. Adult females also occasionally meet and travel with one another. On very rare occasions they groom (a matter of seconds, rather than min-

utes!), touch one another, hold hands, and hug, as well as occasionally chase each other or fight. On one occasion when two adult females held hands, I was fortunate to know their life histories. One was the adult daughter of the other female, her mother, now a grandmother. Even though they shared part of their ranges, I had not seen them meet in ten years. Perhaps this long separation occasioned what was for wild orangutans an emotional interlude. Similarly, I saw adult females who had been friends in adolescence travel together for days at a time.

Adolescent females are downright gregarious compared to their parents. They occasionally travel with their mothers and younger siblings, with whom they sometimes play. Once we captured a wild adult female (who was not part of the regular study group) for medical treatment and had to separate her from her small juvenile son. We put them in two cages just far enough apart that they couldn't touch.

The wild female's adolescent daughter, who traveled with them on and off, located her mother and brother, and then spent a part of every day monitoring the situation from adjacent trees. A day after the capture, the adolescent daughter came down from the trees to the cage where her younger brother was sitting. For almost half an hour the wild adolescent orangutan repeatedly tried, very gently, to take her brother out of the cage. It was impossible for her to slip him through the metal bars. Apprehensive of people watching her from afar, she climbed back into the trees where she vocalized her frustration loudly in the direction of the human observers. All of her subsequent rescue efforts were also centered on her brother, not her mother. Some days later, when the time came to release the mother and juvenile, we took the juvenile and held him next to a tree. The wild adolescent rushed down the tree trunk, snatched her brother, placed him on her side and carried him off into the canopy. Although we released the mother immediately afterwards, she did not retrieve her son from his older sister until a few hours later. The older sister's apparent love for her baby brother brought tears to my eyes. Had she been human, she could not have shown greater care and concern for him.

Subadult males are also somewhat gregarious, but they associate primarily with females, both adolescent and adult. In rare instances they travel with other subadult males, but these associations fall apart if they do not encounter a female. Unlike adult males, subadult males do not avoid each other or fight. However, they usually avoid adult males. The main exception is consorting adult males. Subadult males frequently stalk the consorting pair and sneakily mate with the female while the adult male is distracted or briefly moves away. Some of these matings are clearly forced, others are not. However, most subadult male copulations are forced: rapes in human terms. Although adolescent females do not act proceptively (in human terms, seductively) with subadult males, they generally do not

Princess (right) now spends most of her time in the forest. Here she rests with infant Pan (center) and juvenile daughter Peta. Princess recently became a grandmother when Peta gave birth to a son. Princess's oldest son, Prince, died tragically during adolescence.

object as strongly as adult females do when mated with by subadults. Their protests sometimes seem pro forma, almost as if to test the male. I have seen adolescent females continue plucking and eating fruit, an apparently bored look on their face, while a subadult male copulated with them. The same adolescent females behaved quite differently when they were encouraging a cheekpadded male to mate with them! In this case, it was the male who continued feeding as the adolescent female undulated near him, trying to attract his interest.

Most copulations by fully adult cheekpadded males take place during consortship with a willing female. Of 30 such copulations initially witnessed in my study, only one was resisted. Adult males are interested in attracting and guarding receptive fertile females. For this reason, they are relatively selective in their choices and may reject small eager adolescent females with the too-white faces indicative of youth who have not yet attained full size. These females are less likely to become pregnant. Adult males also will ignore adult females with small dependent young. In the wild, adult cheekpadded males seemed to be able to somehow sense the reproductive status of the female immediately. This contrasts sharply with more inexperienced subadult males who frequently grab a newly encountered female's legs and sniff her genitalia obsessively as if to ascertain her reproductive status, and against all protest, subadult males may forcibly copulate with females carrying small infants. These forced copulations usually entail long struggles between the protesting adult female and the insistent subadult male. I never saw infants harmed in these protracted battles but the copulating pair sometimes ended up mating on the ground which is unusual. This may be the origin of the local Melayu belief that not only do orangutans copulate face to face (as seems to be the case even in trees), but that they must come down to the ground to do it.

No social association between adult males and other lone males has ever been seen. The only times that cheekpadded males have been observed together with subadult males, females were present. When adult males, females, and subadult males have been seen together, the subadult male usually stays a considerable distance away from the adult male.

In fact, male-male competition seems to be one of the organizing factors of a cheekpadder's life. I once read that one of the characteristics typifying Americans is that they play for keeps. It is also true that adult male orangutans play for keeps! If there are two adult males in the presence of a sexually interested adult female, a chase or combat is inevitable. Combat may last a few minutes or a few hours or any time in between. Usually these fights involve bouts of grappling in the canopy and on the ground, with the males biting each other's hands, face, cheekpads, head, ears, shoulders, backs, and feet (especially if one male turns tail and runs), interspersed with longer periods during which the males sit or stand facing each other,

sometimes less than one or two feet apart, staring intently, literally not blinking. There is evidence that, as a shortcut, we judge the size of the body from the size of the head. These staring contests are probably one of the reasons why orangutan males developed cheekpads; cheekpads enhance the size of the head, and the larger the pads, the larger the appearance of the head, and the more powerful the males appear overall.

A typical combat begins with two males sitting some distance apart and staring intently at one another. Sometimes they even stare off into space. Sometimes they move toward each other, but often they are so lethargic that I wonder if a combat will actually occur. But once they engage one another, the ferocity of these combats is not to be underestimated. The wounds of combat are frequently considerable, for both the loser and the winner. After a combat the leaf litter of the forest floor may be covered in drops of blood. (Orangutans are not big bleeders; if they were human, their wounds would be gushing blood.) Adult males are distinguished by their disfigurements, which are probably a result of fights with other males. They have missing, stiff, or gibbled fingers and/or toes, missing eyes, and torn ears, lips, or cheekpads. They may even have puncture wounds all the way to the bone. One postprime adult male had a broken canine. Another had a protruding canine that might have been a result of combat.

Adult males are much more tolerant of subadult males. The mere presence of a lone subadult male is not always enough to trigger an immediate aggressive response. All this, of course, changes when females are present. Then adult males will chase subadults away very aggressively. Sometimes while he is chasing a subadult male, a second subadult male will race in and copulate with the adult male's consort!

I once watched a film of wild chimpanzees from Gombe and noticed an occasional male briefly bobbing up and down. After the lights were turned back on, I asked Jane Goodall what the chimpanzees were doing. She looked mildly astonished and said they were mating. I had entirely missed the action! Orangutans, in contrast, copulate for much longer periods of time. Although subadult males may take only a few minutes to accomplish their act, adult male orangutans may copulate for half an hour—and seem exhausted afterward.

After a female becomes pregnant, which is indicated by her swollen genitalia, she gets a respite from the attentions of males. After she gives birth to a single infant, she carries him or her for the next five years as she moves from tree to tree. They are, I believe, the best mothers in the world.

Multiple births are common among many animals but not in orangutans. While no orangutan twins have been observed in the wild, about one out of ninety natural pregnancies produces twins among captive orangutans, the same percentage as with humans. As for frequency of birth, among the mammals, many of larger size where singletons are the norm, the mother bears

Kusasi, as a subadult male, and another subadult male play-fight in the trees overlooking Camp Leakey. Although this is play, the subtext is to sort out dominance relations for the future.

offspring as frequently as once every one or two years. The orangutan is different, even from the other apes. As I eventually discovered, no other wild mammal gives birth so rarely. A wild orangutan female at Tanjung Puting, on average, gives birth only once every eight years.

Orangutan pregnancy lasts about eight months. Compared to other mammals, orangutans grow very slowly. Indeed, compared to other nonhuman primates, all the great apes are developmental laggards. Perhaps a long period of growth and dependency is required because the great apes have so much to learn and depend so much on it in their adaptations.

With the exception of some prosimians, most nonhuman primate mothers (with fathers occasionally sharing the duty) carry their offspring on their bodies after they are born. Nowhere is this attachment so intense and long-lived as among wild orangutans. For the first six months of his or her life, the infant seems literally glued to the mother. The youngster may crawl around the mother's body but never leaves mother except perhaps when the mother lies down in her night nest. The infant may lay down touching her. Then, sometime after the first six months of life, the little one takes the first tentative steps away from his or her mother.

By the end of the first year, the infant seems comfortable a few feet away from mother, but still appears weak-kneed and tentative, and is most at ease hanging from mother's body or suspended from a twig near her. By the end of the second year, an infant's motor skills have improved appreciatively, although his or her weight and height have increased relatively little. By the third and fourth years, the infant has entered the equivalent of a human toddler's "terrible twos." Although the infant still clings to its mother when she moves, the moment she stops in a tree, the infant is off, playing, exploring, and sometimes even foraging. Not until the infant's fifth year will the offspring finally travel on its own, following the mother from tree to tree. Even then, a mother still occasionally carries the infant who is still suckling at her breast.

Wild orangutan infancy is probably the most idyllic of all primate childhoods. First and foremost, an orangutan infant does not share his or her mother's attention, body, or nipple with any other creature. Although an older offspring may be traveling with the mother and infant, the older sibling is usually some distance away, does not nurse, and does not share the night nest with the rest of the family. For the infant, an older sibling is an occasional diversion and sometimes a welcome playmate, but if the older sibling tries to carry the infant or plays too hard, mother immediately intervenes. Such intervention is rarely necessary, however, because the older sibling is almost invariably gentle and patient.

Neither does the infant share his or her mother's attention with "daddy," because males do not travel with adult females and their dependent young. Single motherhood is the norm.

Orphans all, three infant orangutans cling to each other for comfort at a reha-bilitation site in Tanjung Puting National Park.

RIGHT
Kusasi gently cradles the head of his favorite consort partner in his enormous hand. Like gorillas, orang-utans are highly sexually dimorphic: Adult males are twice the size of females and display cheekpads on the side of their faces, which expand to the size of the head. Cheekpads may also have an auditory func-tion, but that hypothesis is not yet tested.

After impregnating a female, the adult male quickly moves on in search of other females. He may return years later to consort with the same female again, but otherwise there is no visible bond between adult males and females. An adult female may move into a fruit tree where a former consort is feeding but otherwise avoids all contact with adult males. She also tries to evade most subadult males. I remember an adult female running over a quarter of a mile on the forest floor to avoid an approaching subadult male. I was only able to keep up with her by following her juvenile son moving through the trees.

For the six or seven years that it takes the adult female to wean her offspring, adult males will be the individuals she least encounters. Very occasionally, an adult male orangutan will approach a mother and infant, but this interlude is always brief. Or sometimes a cheekpadded male can be glimpsed loitering in the distance. But most often the rarely seen mature males make their presence known with their majestic long calls. However, once she again becomes receptive, the males begin to congregate, first the subadults and then at least one or two adult males.

Although captive orangutans have given birth as young as seven years of age, wild females generally give birth to their first young when they are 15 or 16 years of age. This slow growth and development are consistent with the orangutan's long life span, approximately 60 years in captivity.

Orangutans are among the smartest of animals, demonstrating cognitive abilities that are not seen in other nonhuman primates with the exception of the African apes. In captivity these abilities include recognizing themselves in mirrors, symbolic communication, role reversal, and tool making and tool use. In the wild, orangutans use tools: they make nests for sleeping; they use fans of leaves or branches as overhead covers; they use branches as whisks to chase away stinging flying insects; they crunch handfuls of leaves to wipe their faces; and toss snags (branchless dead trees) to accentuate their long calls or to destroy that nuisance of a human observer. I've seen all this and more in Tanjung Puting. I saw a wild adult male break off a branch and use it as a stick to scratch his behind, and I've also seen an adolescent female break off a branch and insert it inside a hole in a tree trunk, almost in the manner of a probe. I've seen wild orangutans process food with very sophisticated manipulations that required cognitive ability at a level with making and using tools. But only at Suag Balimbing in Aceh, Sumatra, did some orangutans consistently make and use tools in foraging contexts: extracting insects or honey from tree holes and prying seeds from hard-shelled fruit. Orangutans are brilliant botanists: their abilities to remember trees while traveling and to recognize fruit, leaves, and flowers would probably put most humans to shame.

Like chimpanzees, and probably like most large-brained mammals, orangutans learn from each other, and certain

behaviors become common within a population. They also learn much from their mothers and other orangutans they come into contact with in their long lives. Most of the researchers who have studied wild orangutans agree that orangutans have what we might call culture. Yet just as we are coming to understand wild orangutan behavior, their ecology, genetics, and culture, orangutans themselves as populations in the wild are facing potential annihilation and extinction. Massive habitat destruction of the old growth forests of Borneo and Sumatra have made the wild orangutans' future bleak.

According to current estimates, less than 40,000 orangutans remain in the wild, with approximately 30,000 in Borneo and approximately 7,000 in Sumatra. I realized how close orangutans are to the edge when I visited North Sumatra. One of my Indonesian graduate students, Renie Djojoasmoro, had studied the population in a local reserve. After a year's work, she had concluded that the reserve and the adjacent forest held a population of only 16 orangutans. On this visit, after several days of intensive searching, we found only one orangutan nest. Farms and fields intruded into the reserve. Even as we climbed higher up the mountainside, we came across newly planted cassava fields in the forest. The Forestry Department official with us explained that the local people were just cementing their land claims within the reserve. The local government, almost in defiance of the national government a thousand miles away in Jakarta, had unilaterally slashed the size of the reserve, with no reaction from officials in Jakarta. It reminded me of an old Chinese proverb about regional rulers in China's far-flung provinces governing as they wished, "The mountains are steep and the Emperor is far away."

What truly shocked me was my student informing me that the number of orangutans outside of Aceh had actually been overestimated. She suggested that perhaps as few as 400–500 individuals survived in the province of North Sumatra. By contrast, in the forests of Tanjung Puting National Park in Borneo orangutans seem to pop up out of the woodwork. During a mile walk, I might easily spot 20 or 30 orangutan nests. While surveying for wild orangutan nests, I find it almost impossible to avoid running into orangutans. Tanjung Puting National Park itself probably holds a population of 6,000 wild orangutans, making this one of the largest wild orangutan populations on earth. This one population probably dwarfs each of the remaining Sumatran populations and is larger than any other single Bornean population. Despite inroads by illegal loggers and miners, natural (and human-made) disasters, conflict within and between the Indonesian Forestry Department and local communities, Tanjung Puting's forests remain a haven for wild orangutans, testimony to the power of the idea that concentrating resources and attention to enable local people to protect their own forests is a successful strategy, one that we have employed over the last thirty years.

For the semisolitary orangutan, an infant's only playmate is often his or her mother.

THE END OF EDEN

The clock is standing at one minute to midnight for great apes.

KLAUS TOPFER

It is my firm belief that in fifty years there will be no viable population of apes in Africa.

JANE GOODALL

WHEN I FIRST ARRIVED IN KALIMANTAN almost 35 years ago, the great forest, vast, fecund, and seemingly impregnable, stretched endlessly across the island of Borneo. Kalimantan, the Indonesian part of Borneo, takes up about three-quarters of the island and is the orangutan's main homeland, although orangutans are also found on the neighboring island of Sumatra.

The majority of Borneo's people live on the coast. In the interior, Dayak villages hug the riverbanks as they have for thousands of years, isolated by the steep hills and valleys that slice through parts of the island. Yet much of Kalimantan, especially the coastal areas and deltas where mighty rivers empty into the sea, is low and swampy. From the air, the lowland forests and swamps of Tanjung Puting National Park resemble an endless ocean of green stretching to the distant horizon.

When I first arrived, over 90 percent of Kalimantan consisted of primary tropical rain forest, the world's second-largest continuous expanse of tropical rain forest after the Amazon Basin. Some of the tallest trees in the world, 300 feet and higher, were found in its rugged hills and deep swamps. But now Borneo's forest is in retreat, under relentless pressure from the forces of the global economy and of political agendas spawned by the elite. As the world enters the twenty-first

OPPOSITE
The Virunga Volcanoes, home to the mountain gorillas, one of the most endangered primate populations in the world, straddle three different countries— Uganda, Rwanda, and the former Zaire, Democratic Republic of Congo (DRC).

RIGHT
A moth in the tropical rain forests of DRC signals the biodiversity of this large African nation. Along with Indonesia and Brazil, DRC has one of the three richest ecosystems in the world with millions of species, many unknown to science.

century, the great apes, like so many traditional peoples, have become another victim of global and local economics, long-lasting insurgencies, and wars that are, at least partially, simmering legacies of colonial history and bitter modern rivalries for control over increasingly valuable and scarce resources, exacerbated by expanding populations and loss of traditional lifeways. Like a high-speed locomotive with no one at the controls, the world's global economy speeds recklessly into the future, overwhelming everything in its path, destroying habitats willy-nilly and accelerating the extinction of plants and animals, as well as the destruction of traditional human communities and societies that characteristically sheltered the ecosystems in which millions of species resided. The ethical and moral consequences of this oblivious destruction are incalculable, as are the practical consequences for the future.

A former real estate broker, Charlotte Lowell Grimm, once explained to me that there are only three rules in real estate: "location, location, location." Upon rolling it over in my mind, I realized that the three equivalent rules for conservation are "habitat, habitat, habitat." Although chimpanzees venture into dry open areas and gorillas exist on the edge of plantations, nonetheless all the great apes are tied to forest and woodlands. None can exist permanently in the absence of trees. When all is said and done, when other short-term dangers are taken into account, the greatest overall threat to all the great apes is loss of habitat. It is this loss that propels the other threats such as the bushmeat industry and emerging infectious diseases that, in the end, may provide the coup de grace for great ape populations in the wild.

Deforestation is not a modern phenomenon. Trees are a dynamic resource that increase or decrease depending on natural events and human activities. Ever since humans began cultivating land, about 8,000 years ago, the world's forests have been shrinking. Originally about 48 percent of the world's surface was forested. Now this figure is about 29 percent. But this estimate is inflated by the inclusion of "fake forests" or plantations and by degraded (not climax) forests. Between 1990 and 2000 the area of forest cover around the world decreased at a rate of approximately 25 million acres per year. But this rate of net change in forest cover was not evenly distributed over the planet.

A much larger percentage of tropical forests has been lost than forests in other regions. During the decade ending in 2000, 2 percent of the world's forest was lost but within the tropics 5 percent of forest was destroyed. If Indonesia's forests continue to be converted at the current rate of 3.2 million acres per year, there will be no more forests in Indonesia by the year 2081. But it is likely that the rate of destruction could increase, destroying forests even sooner.

Some countries have suffered near total destruction of their forests. In Africa, the country of Togo was originally 33 percent forest and had populations of western chimpanzees; in 2000 only 2 percent of land surface was left forested. It is not surprising that the western chimpanzee recently went extinct there. Sumatra is the second homeland of the wild orangutan in Indonesia. Satellite photos taken between 1982 and 1990 show that about a third of Sumatra's forests disappeared during that period. One hesitates to think about how much more forest has been destroyed in Sumatra since 1990! These examples indicate that, if the processes leading to forest loss are left unchecked, the unthinkable may occur and, except for small pockets, great ape habitat may disappear.

Uganda, homeland of both gorillas and robust chimpanzees, was once 70 percent forest; as of 2000, less than 17 percent of Uganda's total land area is covered by forest. Rwanda, blessed with the mountain gorillas studied by my Leakey sister Dian Fossey, was originally 36 percent forest, now only 12 percent of Rwanda is covered by forest. These figures are even grimmer for countries in West Africa. In Sierra Leone, a country recently ravaged by an unspeakably brutal civil war, the forest originally covered 100 percent of the total land area. Now only 15 percent represents forest or woodlands. The trend is the same all over sub-Saharan Africa.

The prognosis for great ape populations in the wild is bleak. As habitat loss continues, great ape populations decline and fragment, creating increasingly smaller populations that are vulnerable to local catastrophes and random events such as fire or disease. Gorillas provide a frightening example of how populations can decline. Like orangutans, gorillas were added to the US endangered species list in 1970. The largest gorilla subspecies, found in six countries, is the western lowland gorilla; approximately 94,500 of whom are left in the wild. These gorillas have been classified as "endangered." Ironically, compared to other gorilla populations, western lowland gorillas as the "lucky" ones!

The Cross River Gorilla, found only in Nigeria and Cameroon, has the lowest population of any of Africa's great apes. With only 150–200 individuals left in the wild, this subspecies is critically endangered. The better known and also critically endangered mountain gorilla is only found in the Virunga Volcano region of Uganda, Rwanda, and DRC. A decade ago the mountain gorilla population was estimated to number about 620 individuals. Grauer's Gorilla, restricted to the eastern DRC, has been in steep decline for some time; in 1998 perhaps 16,000 individuals were left. Half this population lives in one national park, Kahuzi-Biega, where recently as many as 70 percent of the gorillas could be dead from disease. The gorillas outside the park are probably in a worse situation.

Aside from habitat loss, what is causing the precipitous decline in gorilla populations? The answer is the bushmeat trade: the slaughter and sale of wild animals for human consumption on a commercial scale. Conservationists didn't see it coming; they were blindsided. One reason is that few Western conservationists are permanently stationed in the outback of African villages and logging camps. Karl Ammann, the distinguished wildlife photographer who lives and travels in Africa, alerted the world to the dreadful fate facing all mammal species in West and central Africa. The increasing commercialization of the bushmeat trade seems to be the most immediate threat to the survival of the African great apes. Again, the bushmeat trade is tied to habitat destruction. As gorilla ranges come under increasing logging pressure, the infrastructure of once remote areas is built up, and the bushmeat trade becomes commercialized on such a grand scale that entire gorilla populations have been eaten into extinction.

Some conservationists accused Karl of "sensationalizing the issue" and being "counterproductive," aggravating African governments that prefer "quiet and diplomatic exchanges." Until recently, for example, many African nations preferred to keep the spread of AIDS within their borders secret. Other conservationists were reluctant to criticize what was still seen as traditional African practice. Karl documented the fact that the killing of gorillas and chimpanzees for meat had become a large-scale commercial activity throughout vast areas of Africa. One commercial African hunter openly admitted that he and his two pygmy assistants kill approximately 50 gorillas per year. He also mentioned needing to fulfill the Christmas demand for bushmeat, including specific orders for gorilla meat. Multiply this hunter only ten times and 500 gorillas go into the cooking pot per year. Multiply him just 100 times and 5,000 gorillas vanish from the wild in a year. Wild gorilla populations simply cannot sustain this level of damage for very long without going extinct.

The arrival of the global economy caused a traditional African practice, subsistence hunting, to explode into a profitable industry. In central and West Africa over the entire range of the lowland gorilla, hunting for bushmeat is customary practice. Unfortunately for gorillas, their meat has traditionally been regarded as a delicacy. But until recently, the human population in this region was sparse and the impact on great apes small. What turned bushmeat into a big-time operation was large-scale commercial logging. European logging companies, which had recently begun large-scale operations in Africa, saw big savings in either employing local hunters to supply their staff and kitchens with bushmeat taken from the Europeans' forest concessions or in simply buying the meat from local hunters. Bushmeat is the meat of choice for Africans who can afford it. They like its strong, gamey taste. It is actually more expensive than the meat of domestic animals such as cattle or pigs. Although other sources of animal protein are available, local cultural attitudes limit the alternatives. In addition, local wars and civil unrest have flooded parts of Africa with cheap weapons. No longer are hunters limited to traditional weapons

for their expeditions into the forest. Assault rifles have replaced spears, bows, and arrows. Hunters prefer large, mature animals. But one by-product of the bushmeat trade are the orphaned infant great apes who enter the pet trade, being sold at prices slightly more than the price of the meat on their bones.

As the European logging companies built roads into previously inaccessible forests, new opportunities became available for subsistence hunters and others to sell bushmeat for cash in the markets of distant towns and cities. Logging trucks become a convenient means of transporting bushmeat as well as live infants for the pet trade. The logging roads and the logging itself result in continuing fragmentation of the habitat, putting further pressure on gorilla populations. Furthermore, warfare and other modern encroachments led communities who once had taboos against hunting and eating gorillas, to abandon traditions.

Karl Ammann estimates that at least 700 lowland gorillas are killed and eaten in the commercial bushmeat market every year. These figures are probably conservative. Other conservationists suggest the figure is actually 3,000 to 5,000 per year. Captive gorilla infants are, unfortunately, fragile and usually do not survive the deaths of their mothers—or sometimes whole family groups—for very long. But a few infants survive long enough to be taken to coastal towns and commercial centers where they are put up for sale. The extent of the killing is large enough that about 40 gorilla orphans become available each year in Congo-Brazzaville alone.

Being hunted for your flesh is bad enough. But what happened to gorillas in the wake of the bushmeat crisis may even be worse. Ebola is a usually fatal viral disease that has no known cure nor proven vaccine. Ebola was named after the river in the DRC where it was first discovered and where a 1995 epidemic killed 250 people before the outbreak in the town of Kikwit was contained. It is the Dracula of disease, a reverse vampire that kills you by eating through your veins and arteries and causing your blood to seep through your pores and out of your organs through every single orifice of the body. Death usually follows. A few survive but over 90 percent of victims, including great apes, die within 7 to 21 days of infection. Where Ebola comes from is unknown. Its natural reservoir is unknown. Birds, bats, and insects have been suspected. First identified in 1976, there are three known fatal strains—Zaire, Sudan, and Ivory Coast. The virus is extremely infectious and spreads through contact with bodily fluids, such as a handshake, a kiss, or coughing and sneezing.

Ebola is decimating gorilla populations. Spanish primatologists had been studying gorillas for nine years at Lossi Gorilla Sanctuary in the Congo Republic. Tragically, all eight gorilla families observed since 1994 have vanished. The primatologists are convinced that the gorillas were decimated by Ebola, not poaching. The first that anyone knew that something was

Timber, bound for international markets, is loaded onto a ship at the bustling port of Samarinda in East Kalimantan. East Kalimantan, with its oil, liquid gas, and timber, is one of the richest provinces in Indonesia. Unfortunately, much of the timber trade is illegal and the forests are being destroyed at an increasingly rapid pace.

dreadfully wrong was when six lowland gorillas from one family group were all found dead, along with numerous antelopes and monkeys, near the village of Lossi. Tissue samples taken from the dead animals confirmed that Ebola was the culprit.

The Lossi Gorilla Sanctuary is close to Odzala National Park, which has one of the highest known densities of lowland gorillas in Africa. If Ebola reaches Odzala, the results would be catastrophic for gorillas. Ebola seems to be spreading eastward. The deadly disease has apparently wiped out gorillas in the Minkebe Forest in Gabon and could already be responsible for the deaths of thousands of chimpanzees and gorillas in equatorial Africa. The only positive note is that Ebola has not yet touched the mountain gorillas whose small numbers make them extremely vulnerable to extinction.

The relationship between the transmission of Ebola to human populations and the bushmeat trade is provocative. In a 1996 outbreak, 13 people in Gabon fell ill with Ebola after butchering a dead chimpanzee they had found in the forest. A December 2001 outbreak of Ebola in Gabon may have been the result of people eating a dead gorilla. In many other instances, the outbreak of Ebola in humans followed the deaths of apes and other animals in forests nearby and contact between hunters and great ape carcasses. This relationship is not surprising since Ebola is transmitted through contact with bodily fluids from infected individuals. In human populations, the very virulence of the disease helps contain it because victims don't live long enough to infect many people and the fear of the disease is so great that African authorities put villages under quarantine almost immediately when an outbreak occurs. Unfortunately, such quarantines and monitoring are difficult to put into place for gorillas in the wilds of equatorial Africa. Humans are the major source of spreading Ebola among humans. But it could be that the social nature of the African great apes promotes the spread of Ebola among gorillas and chimpanzees. Also, it is likely that environmental changes, such as massive human encroachment on great ape habitats, the tropical forest, have brought chimpanzees and gorillas on one hand and the Ebola virus on the other, into more contact. The dramatic mortality rates and the lethal nature of the disease indicate that some event or events have served to trigger the emergence of Ebola as a major cause of great ape mortality in the wilds of Africa.

Ebola and commercial hunting for bushmeat have not just decimated wild gorilla populations but also chimpanzee populations. Frequently published and cited estimates of between 100,000 to 200,000 chimpanzees in the wild may or may not be correct; nobody really knows. But what is apparent is that chimpanzee numbers, like gorilla populations, have declined significantly in recent years due to the bushmeat trade and Ebola outbreaks. Chimpanzee populations have certainly declined by more than 66 percent in the last three decades

ABOVE
It breaks one's heart to see baskets of brutally butchered chimpanzees heading out for a market in the West African country of Cameroon. Some ethnic groups in Cameroon eat more meat—primarily bushmeat—than the average person anywhere in the industrialized world.

LEFT
A tiny orphan chimpanzee with pitiful eyes is for sale in Cameroon and will probably not survive very long. The sale of great ape orphans is banned in many countries in Africa but continues unabated as a result of the bushmeat trade.

OPPOSITE
An orphaned gorilla at a sanctuary in Cameroon now has a chance at survival. The bushmeat trade in the Congo Basin has hit gorillas hard.

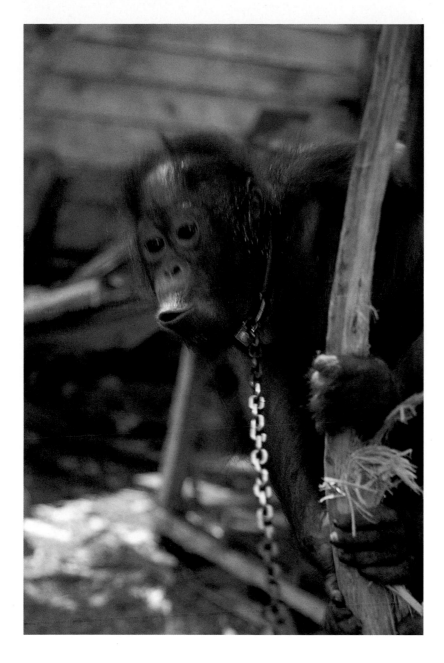

from 600,000 to fewer than 200,000 individuals. The most threatened chimpanzees are the Western and the Nigerian chimpanzee subspecies. They have already become extinct in the West African countries of Togo, Benin, and Burkina Faso. Chimpanzee populations in three other West African countries, Senegal, Guinea-Bissau, and Ghana, number only in the hundreds and are on the edge of extinction. All chimpanzees in western and central Africa are threatened by deforestation, capture for the pet trade, and biomedical research. Recent human population explosions in West Africa have made the situation even more dire. The most current estimates indicate that there are 4,000 to 6,000 Nigerian chimpanzees, perhaps 21,300 to 55,600 Western chimpanzees, 62,000 Central chimpanzees, and 96,000 Eastern chimpanzees left in the wild.

The first documented outbreaks of Ebola in chimpanzees occurred in 1992 and 1994 in the Tai Forest of the Ivory Coast. The chimpanzees were part of a study population observed for many years by Christophe and Hedwige Boesch-Achermann and their colleagues. The two Ebola outbreaks killed about one-third of the study population. One scientist became infected after touching a dead chimpanzee, but fortunately recovered. What is interesting is that since 1994, there have been no further Ebola outbreaks among the Tai Forest chimpanzees. It is almost like a brush fire that sweeps across the landscape and by burning all the vegetation in its way, is not able to return until the landscape is restored and made vulnerable to fire once again.

Both Ebola outbreaks were seasonal, occurring in late October and November. In 1992 eight individuals disappeared within 12 days and in 1994 twelve individuals disappeared within three weeks from the Tai Forest study population. Not only were young infants killed by the disease, but adults were "hit hard," too. The virus seemed to be 100 percent fatal, for none of the apparently infected chimpanzees survived. Analysis of blood samples from some survivors indicated that they were all negative for the virus. The amount of red colobus meat eaten by an individual chimpanzee seemed to be the best marker for whether or not the chimpanzee became infected with Ebola. Boesch and Boesch-Achermann suggested that the most likely scenario was that chimpanzees infected themselves toward the end of the chimpanzees' hunting season by eating red colobus monkeys who were healthy carriers of the Ebola virus. Chimpanzees seem to avoid hunting visibly sick monkeys. Although the chimpanzee hunting season starts in August, since the Ebola virus apparently kills its host in one or two weeks, it appears that the colobus monkeys must have been contaminated in late October. This scenario indicates that colobus are an intermediate and temporary host, and eating them might be lethal for chimpanzees only during certain periods. Grooming or sexual interaction among the Tai Forest chimpanzees cannot explain the Ebola outbreak, as individuals

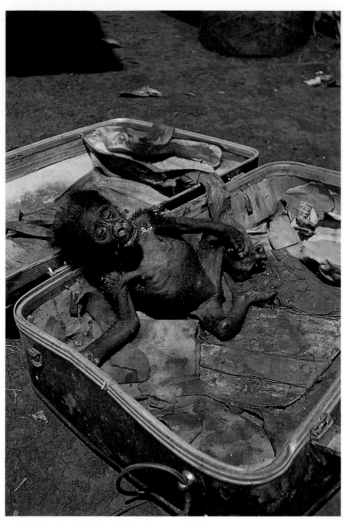

LEFT
A captive chimpanzee juvenile wearing a t-shirt prepares to light a cigarette. Having chimpanzees, or any of the great apes for that matter, parody humans for people's entertainment demeans them and reduces the respect these highly intelligent and sensitive animals deserve from their closest kin, us.

RIGHT
The body of an orphaned gorilla infant, which died the morning this photo was taken, lies in a battered suitcase in a logging camp. No doubt the carrier planned to sell this youngster in the pet trade. This tragedy is multiplied a thousand times throughout Africa.

OPPOSITE
Baby gorilla for sale. The chances that this baby will survive are extremely low. In a matter of days or weeks, she will most likely be dead, just another name-less orphan in the enormous tragedy affecting all great ape species.

who groomed or copulated with a future Ebola victim were not more likely than others to infect themselves.

What caused the sudden emergence of Ebola? One factor changed in the late 1980s: rainfall. For the first time, there were clearly marked dry months. Ecological changes can lead to the emergence of pathogens. Perhaps global climate changes exacerbated by human activity ultimately led to the emergence of Ebola. But as Boesch and Boesch-Achermann point out, human activity much closer to the chimpanzees has more immediate effect on them. Poachers enter the park at night to hunt for duikers and during the day to hunt for monkeys, primarily red colobus.

On a number of occasions poachers shot in the direction of field researchers and the chimpanzees they were following, missing both. But there was direct evidence that the poachers didn't always miss. The researchers found the skull of an adult female chimpanzee with a bullet still inside it. Worse, human encroachment on the park increased substantially during the past decade, with local farmers illegally planting fields inside the park within chimpanzee territories. Chimpanzees start foraging on the farmers' crops such as cocoa beans, which taste very much like the fruits of a wild liana that chimpanzees savor. To the researchers' distress, the study-area chimpanzees began raiding the illegal cocoa fields within their community territory inside the park. Farmers leave in their gardens some of the emergent trees that the chimpanzees will occasionally use for their night nests. The farmers surprise and kill the chimpanzees in their nests when they are still asleep. In 1984 seven males of the study population were probably killed in this manner. The farmers boast of having killed as many as nine chimpanzees on one occasion in this way.

Like gorillas, chimpanzees have not escaped the escalation of the commercial bushmeat trade. For instance, at least half a ton of bushmeat, mostly chimpanzee, gets transported to the capital city of Cameroon in West Africa. In all likelihood, African ape and monkey meat termed "Congolese cuisine" is occasionally available in restaurants frequented by West Africans in cities such as London and Paris. Conservative estimates indicate that over a hundred chimpanzees are eaten a day throughout West and Central Africa.

Nor is Ebola the only disease that affects chimpanzees. In the best known and longest studied wild chimpanzee populations in the world, Gombe and Mahale in Tanzania, chimpanzees have been affected by epidemics such as influenza, polio, and pneumonia that were clearly of human origin. Fortunately these populations recovered over the long term. In a wild chimpanzee population studied in Uganda, chimpanzees regularly move through farmers' fields fertilized with human waste. Under these circumstances, chimpanzees becoming infected with and decimated by some human disease is always a real possibility. East Africa does not have a strong tradition of hunting and

eating primates for food, so Eastern chimpanzee populations, such as found at Gombe and Mahale National Parks in Tanzania and at Kibale in Uganda, are not severely threatened by poaching but rather by habitat destruction and disease. However, many Eastern chimpanzees die from wounds and injuries sustained from being caught in snares set for other animals.

Virtually all studies of wild chimpanzees have taken place within National Parks in Africa. In some cases, such as Mahale, the studies helped upgrade the status of these places to National Parks. But since the protection of animals and habitat is much better in parks and reserves than outside, chimpanzee population declines are more precipitous among chimpanzee communities living in unprotected areas. The Western, Central and Nigerian chimpanzees are extensively hunted for bushmeat all over their habitats. Not surprising, the Eastern chimpanzee may be the highest remaining population. In West Africa, only 6 percent of chimpanzee range falls into protected areas and as few as 25 percent of chimpanzees are found within the boundaries of these protected areas. Clearly, as with gorillas, the future for wild chimpanzees is grim indeed.

Gracile chimpanzees have not escaped the carnage visited upon their robust kin. Found only south of the Congo River, bonobos are trapped by their location in a relatively small, restricted range within a single political entity, the Democratic Republic of Congo (DRC). The DRC has not been a good place for anyone to be. Ravaged by one of the worst conflicts in modern times, a conflict still going on which has killed several million people, the DRC has been racked by seemingly unending civil war and widespread political instability for decades. The Zaire kidnappers who abducted for ransom several students and administrators from Gombe in Tanzania in 1975 came from the same rebel group whose leader, Laurent Kabila, headed a long-term insurgency in his own country. He needed money for guns. Eventually, in the 1990s, Kabila became president of the country whose name he changed from Zaire to DRC. After he was assassinated, his son, still in his twenties, became president. The war continues.

This war has had a horrendous impact on the gracile chimpanzee. In many regions of their range, bonobos were protected from killing by traditional taboos. But human population dislocations and movements of refugees as well as militias and armies shifted people without taboos but with guns into areas bonobos range. Hunting skyrocketed and the sale of gracile chimpanzee infants became rampant. J. Dupain, a bonobo researcher, says that boats traveling down the Lukenie River invariably transport bonobo orphans to Kinshasa, the capital. In the 1980s poachers began taking bonobos on a large-scale for the commercial bushmeat trade. I have seen photos of dead gracile chimpanzees bound and slung from poles held by the smiling uniformed soldiers who had just killed them, photos that broke my heart because the person showing the photos

An orphan infant for sale holds the hair on his head as he instinctively tries to cling to something or someone. For every orangutan orphan who survives the trauma of capture, it is estimated that at least four to eight other orphaned orangutans have died. This infant was fortunate in that he was discovered and placed in a rehabilitation program. It will take an infant such as this one about six or seven years to reach a state of development where he can return to the wild. The program at Camp Leakey has returned over two hundred ex-captive orangutans successfully to the wild at various release sites in and around Tanjung Puting National Park.

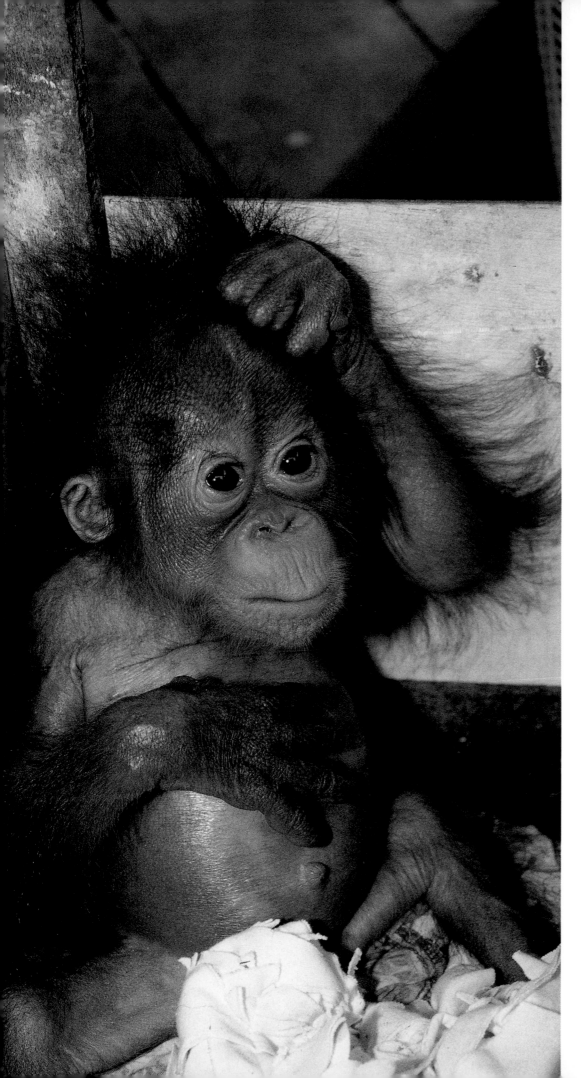

knew not just the soldiers but also the names of the individual dead gracile chimpanzees who were part of populations under study.

At one time the much published and cited guesstimate for the number of gracile chimpanzees in the wild was 15,000 individuals. A higher figure of 20,000 to 25,000 was also cited. In 1995 the Action Plan for *Pan paniscus* put together by experts expressed the fear that "The wild population may already number less than 5,000." Some new data indicate that there may be as many as 30,000 to 50,000 bonobos left in the wild. But these figures do not contradict the strong impression that gracile chimpanzees are on the verge of extinction. A report of a 75 percent decline in Lomako's population since 1998, in an area in the DRC where bonobos have been surveyed in the past, is indicative of the future facing all gracile chimpanzees. In addition, gracile chimpanzee distribution is exceptionally patchy which makes it difficult to understand the exact extent of their range. Whether this patchiness is caused by human impact on habitat, vegetation patterns, or seasonal flooding of forests is unknown.

The paucity of data on gracile chimpanzee numbers, exacerbated by the difficulties of DRC, should not blind us to the fact that of the three African great ape species, the gracile chimpanzees are probably most likely to vanish as a species from this earth. Yes, a few bonobos do exist in captivity but they are the rarest of the great ape species in zoo populations and no substitute, in any case, for the wild animals. The best thing that could happen to gracile chimpanzees is also the best thing that could happen to the war-weary people of DRC—a cessation to the terrible armed conflicts that have ravaged their country for so long.

But the great ape under the greatest threat in the wild, arguably, is the orangutan, the sole survivor in Asia, the only great ape found outside Africa. Disease is not the issue. Semi-solitary in the wild, isolated by its arboreal habits from human populations, quiet, wary, and reclusive, the orangutan is threatened by massive deforestation and the development of its forest habitat for plantations. The two relatively well-off (emphasis on the relative) Asian countries, Indonesia and Malaysia, which were touted as economic mini-tigers in the 1980s and 1990s, have not been helpful to the orangutan's survival as a species. The increased regional autonomy that characterizes Indonesia since the regional financial crisis of 1997, from which Indonesia still has not fully recovered, and the fall of former President Suharto in 1998, does not bode well for the species.

Around the globe the exploitation of tropical rain forests for timber has increased exponentially. The orangutan is cursed by living in forests that are ideal for mass marketing to the industrialized world. Wood from tropical forests in other parts of the world cannot compete in the international timber markets with the woods of Southeast Asia, whose qualities make them commercially ideal. The vast forests of the Amazon Basin include many species with dark, heavy wood that cannot be used for the plywood, peeled veneers, and light particleboard demanded by the world markets. Much to the detriment of orangutans and other native wildlife, the forests of Borneo and Sumatra are a perfect source of wild wood. Emergent trees consist of dozens of dipterocarp species, but these numerous species share common characteristics that allow them to be sold together as only a few major timber classes. This steady supply of wood, organized into a few grades, matches the needs of buyers, who prefer to deal with only a few types of timber. In the last two decades, Southeast Asia has become the world's leading source of tropical timber. Indonesia itself has become the world's largest plywood exporter. Far from being an economic backwater like many African countries, Southeast Asia as a whole began exhibiting annual growth rates of 8 or 9 percent, which made this region an important emerging component of one of the fastest growing economic regions in the world, the Pacific Rim. As was true in the more gradual industrialization of today's developed countries, the modernization of Southeast Asia has had a profound and almost entirely negative impact on wildlife and their habitats.

According to figures released by the Indonesian government in 1990, there are 303 terrestrial protected areas such as reserves and national parks in the country totaling 61,776 square miles. Indonesia is rightfully proud of the vast areas protected by law but, unfortunately, law enforcement in these gazetted areas is very weak. Every single national park in Indonesia that has timber also has illegal logging. Even parks in Java, the most densely populated place on earth, are being illegally logged: truckloads of wood are openly transported out every day. This is not subsistence logging by impoverished local people or dispossessed natives! It is immensely profitable and well-organized international trafficking of valuable timber stolen from national parks for the benefit of local and national elites whose greed seems to know no bounds. But it also stems from the need of local people and migrants who are trying to provide for themselves and their families, and who provide low-cost labor. The net result is that the corrupt elites accumulate more money and power on the backs of small local communities whose forests and futures are destroyed for a relative pittance. There are "boomtowns" in Kalimantan built on illegal logging, but the big money flows to Java and Jakarta and then onward to financial centers outside Indonesia.

Illegal logging is not Indonesia's problem alone. According to the Environmental Investigation Agency (EIA) based in London, illegal logging represents 73 percent of log production in Indonesia, 80 percent in Brazil, and 50 percent in Cameroon. These are three of the world's largest tropical timber suppliers. And Indonesia and Cameroon represent two of the most important great ape habitat countries. The scale of the illegal logging

TOP
Illegal gold mining operations on the northern boundary of Tanjung Puting National Park, Indonesia, pollute the rivers and strip the ground of all forest cover. Thousands of migrants have moved into the area, lured by the prospect of a lucky gold strike. Any wildlife, including orangutans, caught in the area are sometimes killed and eaten.

BOTTOM
Gold mining operations leave behind moonscapes of desolation and devastation from which it will take the forest centuries to recover. Seen from the air are huge white scabs of land inside the forest, serving as a reminder.

OPPOSITE
A starving adult male orangutan, his cheekpads shriveled, bones visible through his skin, walks along, searching for food after the massive devastation of the 1997–98 forest fires that demolished Kutai National Park in East Kalimantan. A government official described the once magnificent cathedral forests of Kutai as an "ashtray." Judging from his condition, this adult male orangutan, like countless others, may not have survived.

is almost beyond comprehension with huge commercial interests at stake. It creates situations where the rule of law breaks down and law-abiding people find it hard to exist without participating in the lawlessness. It thrives on violence, corruption, and greed. And like the most potent narcotic, the ease with which huge profits can be made from illegal timber trafficking becomes highly addictive. I know from personal experience the fury unleashed when illegal timber barons come to believe that they are thwarted and that their addictive profits may be jeopardized. The fury is akin to that of a junkie when someone tries to take his or her heroin away.

The rampant illegal logging of national parks in Indonesia and other great ape habitat countries is fuelled by the massive demand for cheap and plentiful tropical timber in the consuming nations of the Western world, including the United States, European Union, and Japan, as well as mainland China and Taiwan. Japan, in particular, is bloated on timber, importing one-third of internationally traded wood products, more logs and plywood than any other country in the world. Most of Japan's tropical timber imports originate in Malaysia and Indonesia. It is estimated that 50 percent of Japan's tropical timber imports are illegal at source. Japan has more orangutan blood on its hands than any other timber-consuming nation because the illegal timber trade is destroying Indonesia's national parks, the last sanctuary of the orangutans. The most recent entry into this vicious game is the People's Republic of China. China has toughened its stance on logging within its own boundaries. Yet a newly established and rising middle class is clamoring for more goods and furnishing its apartments and homes with quality furniture and accessories. While China's domestic production of timber fell by 97 percent, its log imports increased threefold in a three-year period. China is now in second place as a destination for Indonesian timber, most cut illegally.

The consequences of this timber trade for orangutans and other wildlife are profound. During the last 20 years as much as 80 percent of the orangutans' forest habitat has been lost or severely degraded. The arboreal orangutans, even more so than the more terrestrial African great apes, are highly dependent on trees. Over 90 percent of the orangutans' food comes directly from trees; they spend over 95 percent of their time in trees and they make night nests in trees over 99.9 percent of the time. Without trees, orangutans become refugees in their own land. They have no place to go and no place to hide.

Logging is not the only threat to the tropical rain forest. Agriculture is usually the main reason that these forests are permanently cleared. In Kalimantan the introduction of commercial agriculture is relatively recent. Yet millions of acres of forest have been cleared for palm oil plantations in the last few years alone. The oil palm is a native of Africa. When Jane Goodall began her studies at what was then Gombe Stream

Reserve, she noticed that the wild chimpanzees were attracted to the fruit of the wild oil palms that grew near her camp. Perhaps the palms had been planted by humans, but more likely they were part of the wild flora in the region.

Oil palm is not native to Kalimantan, but once planted it does well in the generally infertile sandy soils. Oil palm seedlings grow rapidly, beginning to produce after about three years. Now, vast areas of forest are rapidly being cleared and burned to plant oil palm. The wild orangutans are trapped. Their forest food sources are gone. Attracted by the inner shoots of the growing oil palms, and later by the fruit itself, many wild orangutans become crop raiders. The result is predictable. When caught in a field, orangutans may be clubbed or stoned to death, for they are now regarded as a pest species. Plantation managers may even put a bounty on orangutan heads or hands. If the victim is a mother, the orangutan bounty hunter can more than double his reward by capturing the offspring and selling the young orangutan on the black market for the equivalent of several months' wages. Most infants and juveniles do not survive in captivity; some become bushmeat. Judging by the ever-increasing number of infant and juvenile orangutans discovered along the roadsides and in local villages, many hundreds of orangutans have died, if not thousands. In the western part of one province in Kalimantan, an evil harvest of hundreds of infant orangutans per year is being reaped.

As large companies move in and local populations become involved in the cash economy, the primary rain forest simply becomes a nuisance. Logging and other roads are driven through to provide access to previously inaccessible places, and the forest is increasingly violated. Aboriginal people are driven out of the forest and settled in towns where, lacking urban skills and formal education, they become the lowest of the underclass. Orangutans and other large animals are killed when they pop into view. Increasing population pressure drives more people into the forest, both locals and newcomers, either as individuals or as part of government-funded development projects, and the traditional shifting horticulture gives way to large-scale forms of permanent agriculture that are incompatible with the maintenance of the rain forest. The balance tips; the equilibrium is lost.

Another grave threat to the existence of the forest is the lure of gold. In some areas of Borneo such as the coastal area where Tanjung Puting National Park is located, there are alluvial fans where great rivers meet in their flow toward the sea. Here, the barren sandy soil beneath the lush rain forest is flecked with gold dust, eroded from the rich gold veins that meander in the rugged mountains of the island's center. Indonesia has become one of the world's leading exporters of gold. Less than half of the 20 tons of gold exported each year comes from licensed mines. The bulk derives from wildcat, independent miners using pans, sieves, and diesel-powered water pumps and hoses to collect a few grams of gold on a lucky day. The damage at any one site may seem small, but collectively these open-air sites damage large tracts of forest in such a way that it will probably take a thousand years for the forest to return. In their desolation, the abandoned sites resemble moonscapes. At the northern edge of the Park, gold fever has transformed once pristine forest into a moonscape of deep, gray pits shrouded by the hovering black fog of pump exhaust fumes. Thousands of people, most newcomers, have settled the area in makeshift towns and villages that seemingly have sprung up overnight.

In addition to clearing trees for gold mining, the use of heavy metals, such as mercury, to separate gold dust from the sand does further terrible damage. These metals run off in the wash water and contaminate the tons of silt that flow into the Sekonyer River as a by-product of the mining. The once-transparent black waters of the Sekonyer River now look like café au lait. Turbid and polluted, the Sekonyer serves both as the highway and bathtub for thousands of people living downstream, who depend on the river for drinking water and hygiene. What damage surface mining will do to these people is as yet unknown, but the already obvious decline in bird life along the river's edge and the paucity of fish in the river foretells a heavy price.

Logging, commercial plantations, and mining have caused up to 80 percent of Borneo's great forest to disappear, to become degraded, or to be replaced by young secondary forest, scrub, or alang-alang grasslands that support only a fraction of wildlife species once present in the forest. I peered into the future of Indonesian Borneo by crossing the border into one of the two states of Malaysian Borneo, Sabah. When I first visited Sabah in 1990, I was amazed by its beauty and astonished by its gas stations, direct dial telephones, faxes, and air conditioned shopping malls with escalators. At that time there were no telephone lines in Pangkalan Bun, the small town near which I lived in Kalimantan Tengah when I was not at Camp Leakey; I still communicated with the outside world by telegrams and air mail. Yet in Sabah an asphalt road ran right up to the gates of the forest reserve at Sepilok that sheltered the world's first orangutan rehabilitation program. I arrived in a city taxi! Palm oil plantations covered the land. I had never seen such vast plantations. There was little space for wild nature outside the parks and reserves. At the conference I was attending, a local dignitary remarked in his speech that the twinkling lights the people of Sabah saw at night were no longer the stars but the navigation lights of passing Japanese timber ships.

The future I saw in Sabah in 1990 came to Kalimantan all too soon. By 1995 many of the ancient primary forests I had visited in the 1970s were gone. Palm oil plantations came within several hundred yards of the Sekonyer River bank on the left-hand side. Local villagers cleared and claimed forest without planting crops just to prevent palm oil plantations from expanding into village land. In another village settled by migrants, most of the villagers became employees of the plantation. Vast palm oil plantations mark the northern boundary of Tanjung Puting National Park and are closing in on the eastern border as well. Crossing Kalimantan Tengah by road indicates how far the plantations have spread. One can go 20 miles and see nothing but oil palms right up to the horizon. Thirty years ago, this was climax rain forest, untouched forest, and home to millions of species, including orangutans and gibbons.

In the last 20 years, terrible disasters in the form of huge fires further destroyed the forests of Borneo. During 1982–83 what was then called the Great Fire of Borneo raged for almost a year. Up to that time, it was the largest forest fire recorded in human history. Over ten million acres of lowland tropical rain forest were incinerated. Supposedly sparked by the numerous small fires local people traditionally light to clear dry rice fields, this great fire was blamed on El Niño, a climatic oscillation that warms the normally cool surface of the eastern Pacific Ocean. The rains that fall on Indonesia during the wet season instead fell into the waters of the equatorial Pacific, causing a prolonged drought. But even then there were whispers that the cause of this great fire was not what people thought it was. Rumors spread that logging companies torched expired concessions to destroy evidence that the required re-planting, mandated by law, had not taken place. But the official cause was laid at the doorstep of traditional shifting cultivators, even though these were the people who took the greatest care with controlling fire.

In 1997 another long drought produced by El Niño caused another colossal forest fire that was fanned by relentless human activity. Massive deforestation, the result of legal and illegal logging and clear-cutting to make way for plantations, produced a disaster of epic proportions. A thick blanket of smoky haze closed airports as far away as mainland Asia. The smoke was so dense and widespread that people in Kuala Lumpur, Malaysia, Bangkok, Thailand, and even Darwin, Australia, felt its effects. President Suharto of Indonesia, in an absolutely unprecedented move, sincerely apologized for the fires to his own people and to the people and nations of the region, possibly unwittingly helping his own demise as ruler a year later. This time there were few rumors as to the origins of the fires; the Minister of the Environment himself cautioned that, according to satellite imagery, 80 percent of the large fires originated in palm oil concessions. Since the cheapest form of forest clearance is fire, it was not surprising that palm oil concessionaires took the opportunity of the drought to clear land for their plantations. While in 1983 the fires had been predominantly in Sabah and East Borneo, in 1997 they spread over the entire island of Borneo. Worst hit was the province

At Taiwan Monkey Park, a captive silverback gorilla "fathers" an orangutan juvenile. Even under the stark conditions of captivity, the gorilla male's instinct for fatherhood and protection finds expression.

of Kalimantan Tengah. Estimates of the damages are probably gross underestimates. This fire was probably even more devastating than the fire of 1982–83.

Apart from the blackened, smoldering landscapes and dense haze, one of the most visible consequences of the fire in Kalimantan Tengah was the flood of orangutans coming into captivity. Many more, especially mothers of infants and juveniles, were slaughtered. A foreign film crew investigating the fires found three captive orangutan infants in less than an hour in Palangka Raya, the provincial capital of Kalimantan Tengah. In one case, the badly malnourished infant's cage was partially covered by the drying pelt of his mother. The illiterate farmer proudly demonstrated his technique for killing orangutans fleeing the decimated smoking forest on the ground. At least these farmers were eating the flesh of the orangutans they slaughtered. The film crew was so shaken that they stopped inquiring about orangutans. A week later another group discovered seven newly captured infants in a small town in the province. Fortunately, all ten infants were confiscated, and plans made to send them to a rehabilitation program.

Rehabilitation, the planned release of ex-captive orangutans back to the wild after strenuous health checks and however long a period of training is necessary for orphans, has been controversial. Scientists, government officials, and conservationists, as well as many people who have never seen an orangutan in the wild, strenuously argue the pros and cons of rehabilitation and the merits of various programs. It reminds one of medieval theologians debating how many angels could dance on the head of a pin. At least the theologians presumably couldn't harm the angels. The preoccupation with rehabilitation is a symptom of the failure to address the underlying causes of the orangutan crisis. Rather than endlessly debating the detailed aspects of rehabilitation programs, we should concentrate on stopping the flow of captive orangutans and the destruction of tropical rain forests in Borneo and Sumatra, the orangutan's only habitat.

Yet rehabilitation's connection with ecotourism (also known as value or nature tourism) is helpful for conservation. The practical reality is the presence of orangutan rehabilitation programs helps protect forests for wild orangutans. Ex-captive orangutans in their natural forest environment attract visitors. Ecotourism has been promoted as at least a partial solution to the problems faced by endangered species. It injects a positive economic element into the equation of conservation. Endangered species earn their keep by attracting visitors. Local people are employed to maintain the sites, to work in facilities established to feed and house the visitors and to guide and guard travelers. A good case is Sepilok. In the early 1990s when I visited, there were 70,000 people visiting the site annually. In Tanjung Puting we were able to grow tourism with the help of Earthwatch, a Boston-based group that found

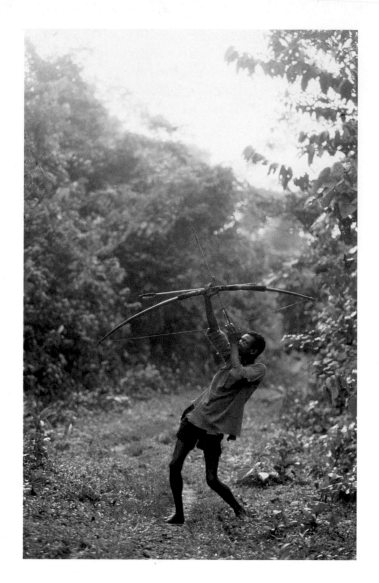

LEFT
A hunter near Wamba, DRC, demonstrates his prowess with a bow and arrow. Traditional hunting has given way to a bustling commercialized bushmeat trade that relies on professional hunters, modern roads and infrastructure, modern weapons such as rifles and machine guns, and access to large urban markets where bushmeat is the meat of choice.

OPPOSITE
Tea plantations and other developments surround Kahuzi Biega, spelling out a difficult future for the endangered gorillas and other wildlife within the park.

volunteers willing to pay their own way to help Camp Leakey's programs, and by Orangutan Foundation International's study groups. This generated employment for local people and helped create institutional and governmental, as well as local, support and commitment for orangutan conservation and protection of the forest. The ecotourists themselves also became goodwill ambassadors for the work being done at Tanjung Puting and, by extension, elsewhere.

Wild orangutan populations are under siege. In Sabah, starving wild orangutans have been encountered at the edge of rubber and other plantations. In Kalimantan Tengah desperate wild orangutans are found and often slaughtered deep within palm oil plantations miles from the nearest wild tree. Like homeless people, homeless orangutans are a nuisance, an eyesore, an uncomfortable tug on the conscience. Society prefers either to turn its back on this population or to eliminate it, whichever is easiest. The simple solution for orangutans and all the great apes—saving tropical forests where great apes make their home—is the most difficult to implement.

There is no doubt that the orangutan stands on the edge of extinction; wild orangutan populations have declined by at least 50 percent in the last 20 years. Somewhere between 25,000 and 40,000 animals are believed to survive in the wild in Borneo and Sumatra. I believe that this figure is somewhat larger but, in reality, what matters is not the absolute number of orangutans in the wild but the fact that their numbers are declining so rapidly that they will be gone in a matter of a few decades. This extinction will not be as complete as, for example, the North American passenger pigeons or heath hens, where not one bird survived.

With hundreds of orangutans in captivity, this extinction will be like that of the European bison. A few herds of semi-domesticated bison survive in forestlands on the Polish-Lithuanian border, sometimes protected by Lithuanian farmers who feed the bison during severe winters. But as an ecological force, the European bison vanished hundreds of years ago. There are no more wild European bison; they have no more impact on nature as a whole.

To save the orangutans and the other great apes, the forest must be preserved—an improbable although not an impossible goal. As a species, we have thrived by achieving what seems to be impossible. Yet here, the possible continues to elude us. In

Market day in a village at the base of the Virunga Volcanoes in DRC demonstrates the human population explosion that is the source of the doom awaiting most great ape populations in Africa.

the end the solution to orangutan extinction will be piecemeal: a patchwork of economic, political, cultural, and social negotiations and compromises. Someday soon there may be no more orangutans except in national parks, reserves, and zoos. One could say that the human species had once again outcompeted one of its nearest hominoid relatives. (And will likely do so with the other great apes who remain). Won't we become lonely on a planet endlessly spinning, contemplating all that once was and all that we once shared with our close relatives, the great apes?

I don't have universal solutions to the problems facing the great apes because universal solutions are not possible. What seems to have worked in the past are individuals and small groups, sometimes even called lone rangers by their critics, who set up field stations or programs in areas and then stay, or encourage their students or associates to stay permanently in the area. Forests and habitat are protected better around these stations and programs, simply because there are eyes to watch and fieldworkers to report to government agencies and others what is happening. When I first went into the field, I was told by the head of the Indonesian government agency responsible for wildlife and forest conservation that he wanted me in Kalimantan Tengah, to be his "eyes and ears" in an area where he had no officials. Since his family came from Sumatra and he had many allies and colleagues there as well as kin, he had no interest in sending me to Sumatra where I originally wanted to study orangutans. Ironically, 20 years later another head of the same government agency asked me to relocate to Sumatra as his envoy and repeat what we had done in Tanjung Puting National Park.

Working with action-oriented smaller conservation organizations as well as publishing articles in the popular media, we helped raise the profile of Tanjung Puting to such a degree that the Park became known round the world. We also worked very hard with various levels of government to enhance the visibility and importance of the Park. The government helped; a world conference for great ape experts in the early 1990s was opened by President Suharto and funded by the Minister of Tourism, Telecommunications and the Post. Ironically, this minister had become acquainted with Tanjung Puting by watching National Geographic Society specials on late-night television while he was Indonesia's ambassador to the United States! Perhaps most important, local government officials began to see that Tanjung Puting was part of their heritage. A powerful Dayak political oganization even put the protection of Tanjung Puting National Park into their oath as one of their missions. The fact that the Orangutan Foundation International funded the employment of over 200 local Indonesians in conservation and forest protection pursuits was very significant for local support. These local Indonesians and their families and kin, who were almost all natives of Kalimantan, formed a vocal constituency for conservation that the local government could not

ignore. In East Kalimantan, Dr. Suzuki had similar success. During the fires of 1997–98, in his absence, his assistants, local villagers, kept his field station and some of his study area free from fire, while all around fires burned out of control in Kutai National Park.

The study area that I established in 1971 is only about 1.5 percent of the park. To protect the northern part of the park in the vicinity of Camp Leakey, since the year 2000 we have worked with local police, park management and forest police, and local communities to physically block the mouths of rivers with chartered boats and armed police officers, as well as with local people to prevent loggers from taking out illegal timber. This has worked so well that all illegal cutting and gold mining in the northern part of the park has stopped 100 percent in the areas served by the river blocks and standing patrols. We also started building guard posts inside the deep forests of the park and stepped up our patrols, increasing the area under protection to approximately 50 percent of the park.

In the beginning of 2003 the president of Indonesia herself, Megawati Sukarnoputri, very aware of Tanjung Puting, and reminded by a letter from 12 US senators of the urgency, ordered the police chief of the Republic of Indonesia to take action and evict all illegal loggers from the remaining 50 percent of Tanjung Puting National Park that was not under our control. Four hundred and fifty men, members of the military and the elite mobile brigades of the police, were sent into the park supported by helicopters. Tanjung Puting became the one national park in Indonesia where illegal logging was eradicated. A few months later the local police shot two loggers who were trying to take previously cut wood out of the park, killing one. Two years later there are still no illegal logging operations being carried on in the park.

In fact, in our area we don't really speak about orangutan conservation but rather about raising employment opportunities for local communities and protecting their resources for the future. The key element has been convincing the government to enforce the law and protect the park, something that was only possible to do with the support of the local police and local communities. In addition, we were able to persuade the Indonesian government to establish another reserve close to Tanjung Puting National Park, which protected more forest. We are using the same approach of local police and community support to rid this reserve of illegal logging and resource extraction. All our struggles to save forest and serve local communities were vindicated when a recent nest survey indicated that our efforts of the last 34 years to protect orangutans in Tanjung Puting has been so successful that the 6,000 wild orangutans estimated to be in the park represent one of the two largest orangutan populations in the world!

But, of course, the big issues for great ape conservation are global and beyond the scope of even major conservation organ-

OPPOSITE TOP
An orphaned bonobo for sale in Kinshasa, the capital of DRC. Unless he or she ends up in a sanctuary, there is no hope for survival. Bonobos are particularly fragile and do not usually survive captivity as motherless orphans.

OPPOSITE BOTTOM
The only real hope for captive African apes, such as these bonobos, is a sanctuary. Here caretakers at a sanctuary in Kinshasa hold the orphaned infants. Like all great apes, bonobo infants need to be carried and touched almost constantly during their first year of life. For orangutans, rehabilitation programs are the main hope for orphaned animals. Yet, only when local people begin to value and care for great ape populations in their own countries, will there finally be genuine hope for the survival of great ape species in the wild.

izations. Population control is a must for developing countries with great ape habitat. Justice and fairness in world trade must allow people in great ape habitat countries to gain economic opportunities that will take them out of rural poverty and into middle-class prosperity. Conservation and environmental education must become mainstream so the next global generation will understand the issues. As long as masses of people in Africa and Asia do not have the economic and other opportunities available in developed countries, they will do what they have always done, live off the land. But today's burgeoning populations devour the landscape and resources unsustainably, and great apes will not survive.

In the last few years, agencies of the United Nations have joined in a strategic alliance with governments, non-governmental organizations (NGOs), and private sector interests to establish GRASP, the Great Apes Survival Project. Only time will tell how successful this new alliance is; nonetheless, it is very hopeful that something at this level would be organized. Dian Fossey would be proud, for one of the people helpful in bringing this about and who is very much involved with GRASP, is Ian Redmond, one of her devoted students who once took a poacher's spear in his arm while working with her to defend mountain gorillas.

However, in the end, we are left with the inescapable conclusion that the main hope for the great apes is the native people of the countries where apes live. Until the political, economic, and intellectual elites join with the "average Joes, Janes, and Mohammeds" of great ape habitat countries in valuing the existence of great apes and forests, there is not much hope. But my last 34 years in Indonesia, including the action of President Megawati in safeguarding Tanjung Puting National Park, and the support of local native communities without which I could not have survived, have convinced me that there is hope and that local people increasingly are beginning to care about the survival of our closest living relatives. It begins in the schools and government offices, but it reaches down into the villages. It is still a small eddy, but it is growing in force and one day it will be a tsunami. Let us hope that great apes can survive until that day.

Page numbers in *italics* refer to illustrations.

The following organizations are among those that are trying to help our great ape kin escape extinction. Please contact these organizations for further information on how you can help.

To my greatest sources of inspiration:

My mother and late father, Filomena and Antanas Galdikas;
my husband, Bohap bin Jalan;
my children, Binti, Fred, and Jane;
and to Davida, Mellie, and Gestok and all their fellow great apes.

Editor: Andrea Danese
Designer: Darilyn Lowe Carnes
Production Manager: Justine Keefe

ISBN 978-1-4351-1009-0

Copyright © 2005 Biruté M. F. Galdikas

Printed and bound in Singapore

10 9 8 7 6 5 4 3 2 1

HNA ▮▮▯▯▯
harry n. abrams, inc.
a subsidiary of La Martinière Groupe

Harry N. Abrams, Inc.
115 West 18th Steet
New York, NY 10011
www.hnabooks.com

Orangutan Foundation International
4201 Wilshire Blvd., Suite 407
Los Angeles, CA 90010
tel: 323–938–6046
fax: 323–938–6047
e-mail: ofi@orangutan.org
website: www.orangutan.org

Orangutan Foundation U.K.
7 Kent Terrace
London NW1 4RP
United Kingdom
tel: 44–20–7724–2912
fax: 44–20–7706–2613
e-mail: info@orangutan.org.uk
website: www.orangutan.org.uk

Australian Orangutan Project
P.O. Box 1414
South Perth
WA 6951
Australia
e-mail: leif@orangutan.org.au
website: www.orangutan.org.au

Sepilok Orangutan Rehabilitation Centre
WDT 2001, Sandakan
Sabah 90000
Malaysia
tel: 60–89–531190
fax: 60–89–531189
e-mail: soutan@po.jaring.my
website: www.sabah.edu.my/
    srmo12.wcdd/BM/menu1.html

Jane Goodall Institute for Wildlife Research, Education and Conservation
P.O. Box 14890
Silver Spring, MD 20911–4890
tel: 301–565–0086
fax: 301–565–3188
e-mail: info@janegoodall.org
website: www.janegoodall.org

Wild Chimpanzee Foundation c/o Max Planck Institute for Evolutionary Anthropology
Inselstrasse 22
Leipzig 04103
Germany
tel: 49 341 99 52 139
fax: 49 341 99 52 119
e-mail: wcf@wildchimps.org
website: www.wildchimps.org

Ngamba Island Sanctuary (Chimpanzees)
P.O. Box 369
Entebbe
Uganda
tel: 256–41–320662
fax: 256–41–320662

Sweetwaters Chimpanzee Sanctuary
P.O. Box 167
Nanyuki
Kenya
fax: 254–176–32408 or
    254–176–32409

Chimfunshi Wildlife Orphanage
P.O. Box 11190
Chingola
Zambia
e-mail: 2chimps@bushmail.net
website: www.chimfunshi.org.za

Pan African Sanctuary Alliance (PASA)
website: www.panafricanprimates.org

Bonobo Protection Fund
Georgia State University Foundation
University Plaza
Atlanta, GA 30303
tel: 404–244–5825
fax: 404–244–5752
website: www.gsu.edu/~wwwbpf/
    bpf.html

The Dian Fossey Gorilla Fund
110 Gloucester Avenue
London NW1 8HX
United Kingdom
tel: 44–20–7483–2681
website: www.dianfossey.org

Dian Fossey Gorilla Fund International
800 Cherokee Avenue, SE
Atlanta, GA 30315-9984
tel: 800–851–0203
fax: 404–624–5999
e-mail: 2help@gorillafund.org
website: www.gorillafund.org

Projet Protection des Gorilles
BP 13977
Brazzaville
Congo
tel: 242–83–73–39
fax: 242–83–73–39
e-mail: 103757.2526@compuserve.com